Attract and
Retain the
Affluent
Investor

Attract and
Retain the
Affluent
Investor

*Winning Tactics
for Today's
Financial Advisor*

Stephen D. Gresham
Evan Cooper

DEARBORN™
T R A D E
A **Kaplan Professional** Company

Vice President and Publisher: Cynthia A. Zigmund
Senior Managing Editor: Jack Kiburz
Interior Design: Lucy Jenkins
Cover Design: Design Solutions
Typesetting: the dotted i

Published by Dearborn Trade, a Kaplan Professional Company

Printed in the United States of America

01   02   03   10   9   8   7   6   5   4   3   2   1

Library of Congress Cataloging-in-Publication Data

Gresham, Stephen D.
    Attract and retain the affluent investor : winning tactics for today's financial advisor / Stephen D. Gresham, Evan Cooper.
       p.   cm.
    Includes index.
    ISBN 0-7931-4433-7 (6×9 hardcover)
    1. Financial planners. 2. Investment advisors. I. Cooper, Evan. II. Title.
HG179.5 .G74 2001
332.6′2—dc21

                               2001000923

Praise for *Attract and Retain the Affluent Investor*

"There is no one in this industry who understands the psychology of the affluent investor better that Steve Gresham. Steve's book will help any financial advisor understand the important protocol of attracting and retaining assets of the affluent investor."

—Frank Campanale, President and
Chief Executive Officer, Consulting
Group, Salomon Smith Barney

"Steve has been a valued advisor to me and our company. We value his insights and find his candor refreshing. He sees the financial world from a unique perspective—he knows *both* the client and the advisor. Financial advisors and industry executives alike can benefit from Steve's insights as they strive to succeed in this ferociously competitive marketplace."

—John Philip Coghlan, Vice Chairman,
Charles Schwab

"Gresham is an expert on today's affluent client. The book is packed with unique insights and actionable advice on how to better serve this complex and growing market by becoming a true wealth manager."

—Michael J. Cemo, President,
AIM Distributors, Inc.

"Steve Gresham and Evan Cooper have put together a practical, concise guide on how to approach the high net worth marketplace. Many books today can take you up to 30,000 feet and point out the trends that will drive our industry for the next decade. This book brings you back down to earth and shows you what you need to do to make those trends work for you."

—Len Reinhart, Chairman and CEO,
Lockwood Financial Group Ltd.

"Stephen has an in-depth understanding of the financial services global marketplace and brings to our financial consultants a reality check of the ultra high net worth client's wants and needs."

—Steven E. Dear, First Vice President, Director of Training and Organizational Development, Merrill Lynch International Private Client Group

"Everywhere we turn in today's financial services marketplace we hear claims of expertise in 'wealth management.' One of the few experts I follow and pay attention to is Steve Gresham. His book, like Steve himself, is sharp, cogent, and to the point. It is *the* road map to success in building and managing a wealth management practice."

—Jack Sharry, President, Private Client Group, Phoenix Investment Partners

"It is not often I can say a book about financial advisory services is impressive, riveting, and intensely readable. But that sums up Gresham and Cooper's new book, *Attract and Retain the Affluent Investor*. When I say they will take you on an exciting journey into your professional future, I mean it. This book is loaded with the telling changes at the margins that translate into significant success."

—Russ Alan Prince, President, Prince & Associates

Contents

Preface

A Time for Change

*T*he decade of the 1990s certainly was a golden age for financial advice. Overall, both clients and advisors succeeded beyond their most optimistic hopes. Robust equity markets propelled the value of client portfolios to record highs, while financial advice givers profited from the booming demand for their counsel.

The new millennium has brought with it a shift in climate. As advice givers, you recognize things have changed, and forces over which you have no control are shaping your future. It's natural you are worrying about:

- An uncertain economy and falling stock prices
- Competition from online services that, while not replacing you, erode your authority
- Competition from former allies, such as accountants
- Competition from your own firm as it develops alternative distribution channels
- Pricing pressure
- The transition to fee-based business and your sense that many of your clients may not choose to switch
- Greater pressure to gather assets
- Whether you are truly your clients' chief financial advisor

But worrying won't answer the basic question: What should you—the successful advisor—do now to prosper in the future?

Over the next several chapters, we're going to answer that question. We're going to give you new ways of thinking about the service model you currently deliver and some practical suggestions—from practitioners who have tried and tested new methods—that will help you adapt your business to serve tomorrow's affluent clients. Without going into too much detail, let's introduce you to several advisors whose stories appear throughout the book. These advisors work at wirehouses, regional and local securities firms, independent brokerages and financial advisory firms, insurance companies, investment banking firms, commercial banks, and trust companies. In many cases, we use their actual names and affiliations; in others, because of compliance issues, we use pseudonyms. Here are some of the advisors you'll be meeting:

- Stephen A. "Tony" Batman, founder of 1st Global, Inc., in Dallas, Texas, who explains why accountants may soon dominate the delivery of financial advice.
- Scott F., a broker in the Boston area, who is taking his practice into the future by transforming himself into a wealth manager.
- Keith G., who has built a practice around charitable giving and who has developed a method for discovering the hidden wishes of affluent business leaders.
- Stephen Grillo, an agent of the Northwestern Mutual Financial Network in Bradford, Pennsylvania, who relates how he transformed himself from an insurance salesman to a wealth advisor.
- Steve H., with a wirehouse in Boston, Massachusetts, who explains how he made the switch to fees—and came to manage $2.5 billion.
- Joe K., an executive with the private wealth management group of one of the nation's largest investment banking firms, who shows how teams can produce results a solo advisor can't.
- George K., who left a career trading futures in Chicago to become a broker in the Midwest and who developed an 11-step process that led him to pare his book.

- Gary Rathbun, a private wealth advisor in Toledo, Ohio, who started in insurance and is now a personal chief financial officer to his clients.
- Chuck R., a wirehouse financial advisor in North Carolina, who learned about a secret fear of affluent clients from an unusual firsthand experience.

What these advisors have in common is an uncommon ability to serve affluent clients. Their experiences and insights can give you the confidence you need to tap this market more effectively. From the start, you can be confident of at least one thing: we will *not* be proposing that you make wholesale changes in the way you do business. First off, you are already successful and have proven that your basic approach to serving clients is working. Second, drastic change of any kind—like going on a radical weight-loss diet—rarely works in the long run. And finally, making just a few small, but strategic, changes at the margins of your business can have the greatest impact of all in increased revenue and earnings.

Over the course of the following chapters, you can expect to find out how to:

- Concentrate your focus and earn more from fewer clients.
- Provide a richer and more complex level of service.
- Increase client satisfaction and loyalty.
- Determine which specialization path is right for you.
- Function less as an investment counselor and more as a wealth advisor.
- Prospect for clients and expand your business with greater effectiveness.
- Enjoy greater career satisfaction.

For successful advisors, finding new ways to attract and retain affluent clients is an exciting journey. Let's begin by examining the psyche of affluent clients and what they want from you.

Acknowledgments

*H*aving written only speeches and magazine columns, I wondered if I would have enough valuable information to share with financial advisors. Those concerns evaporated in the withering stock markets of 2000 and 2001. While Nasdaq prices melted before us, I found new energy and new urgency in our task of sharing the best practices of top advisors. I begin my acknowledgments with you, the buyer of this book, for your vote of confidence in us to provide that information.

The second group of people to thank are those who gave more of themselves to provide me the time—since I had to continue managing a full-time consulting practice. I can't say enough about my partner, Arlen Oransky, and his partner, Christine, who provided support and encouragement even as they assumed extra work responsibilities. Glen Gresham was a patient editor—a tough role for both an accomplished author and father. Phyllis Gresham, my mother, always challenged my assumptions but supported my decisions. More than anyone else, Lisa Gresham provided me the opportunity to write, and I will always be grateful for that gift.

Our clients at The Gresham Company provided insight and encouragement along the way, as well as suggestions for how we could better apply our observations of the financial advisor marketplace: Robyn Howard and all the great folks at AIM; Jack Sharry of Phoenix Investment Partners; Ed Foley and Clark Lee of Prudential; Doug Heikkinen of Charles Schwab; George Yeager of Yeager, Wood & Marshall; Deb Withey of CUNA Mutual; Kathy Klingler and Jason Diamond of Signator Investors; Bruce Johnston and Greg Gloeckner of Conseco; and Connie Chartrand, Kevin Boman, Jim McClocklin, and Steven Dear of Merrill Lynch International Private Client Group were all instrumental in our success as a firm as well as with this book.

I owe a personal debt of gratitude to several professional colleagues who have helped guide me and The Gresham Company as we continue our quest for value in all that we offer to the advisory world. Leo Pusateri is a valued friend and accomplice, Russ Alan Prince is the brightest guy in the business, Chris Davis of the Money Management Institute has no shortage of valuable opinions, and Sydney LeBlanc is a terrific collaborator. In combination with the illustrious names on the back cover of this book, these characters make the job rewarding and fun. Thanks.

Finally, I thank the advisors who have shared their time with us. Your efforts are appreciated by us, by the other advisors whose practices you will aid, and most importantly, by the clients who are so fortunate to have you as their counselors. Yours is the real story.

—Stephen Gresham

Writing a book is not unlike taking photos with a zoom lens. The writer, like the photographer, must be able to change focus—pulling back to see the entire picture and then zooming in to capture fine detail. If the writer is successful, the reader gains something from both views and doesn't get dizzy in the switching process. I was fortunate to have had several people help me try to keep both perspectives in focus.

I join with my coauthor, Steve Gresham, in thanking Arlen Oransky for his invaluable organizational and orchestrating skills that helped me gather the material I needed. I also thank our team at Dearborn—Cindy Zigmund, Jack Kiburz, and company—for their guidance, support, encouragement, and forbearance. Thanks, too, to my colleagues, Bruce Morris, Tom Fowler, and Ed Tiscornia, at the Investment Marketing Group of Thomson Financial, publishers of *On Wall Street* magazine, for supporting my involvement in this endeavor, and to Tom Johnson, editor of *Financial Planning* magazine, for his thoughtful suggestions.

My biggest thanks go to my wife, Sandy Geller. Her contributions of time, understanding, and patience made the book possible. Her other contributions to my life make it all worthwhile.

—Evan Cooper

Chapter *1*

Who Are Today's Wealthy Clients?

| And what drives them?

No matter how wealth is measured, we can say with certainty that a record number of Americans have entered a golden age of affluence. More than 5.35 million U.S. households now can be categorized as having a net worth of at least $1 million (Bill Whitt, *Eyes on the Prize,* VIP Forum, 2000). As affluent as these families are—and remember that the net worth of the median American household, excluding its home, is less than $15,000—what's more astounding is their growth. (See Figure 1.1.) From 1992 to 1995, the number of these elite households grew from 2.82 million to 3.05 million—a compound annual growth rate of 2.6 percent. But from 1998 to 2000, the number of these households grew even faster, going from 4.68 million households to 5.35 million households—a compound annual growth rate of 12.6 percent.

Mark P. Hurley, president and CEO of Undiscovered Managers, a Dallas, Texas–based research firm, calls the bulk of these house-

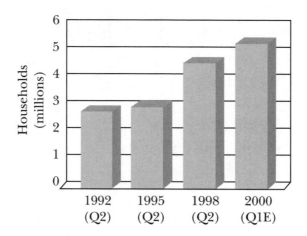

FIGURE 1.1

Number of U.S. Households with Net Worth of $1 Million or More, 1992–2000 (in millions)

(Compound Annual Growth Rate, 1992–1995 = 2.6%; 1995–2000 = 12.6%)

Source: VIP Forum, *Eyes on the Prize.*

holds—those with a net worth between $1 million and $10 million—the "semiaffluent" ("The Future of the Financial Advisory Business and the Delivery of Advice to the Semi-Affluent Investor," Undiscovered Managers, 1999). Very wealthy households, by his definition, are those where the net worth exceeds $50 million. These five million semiaffluent households, he says, are the chief targets of brokerage firms, banks, insurers, independent planners, and other financial services providers.

For financial professionals who want to set their sights higher than the semiaffluent, the growth in the number of "decamillionaire" households—those with a net worth in excess of $10 million—has been growing at the even faster rate of 13.2 percent a year. Between 1995 and 2000, the number of these households has grown from almost 181,000 to 326,500 households. (See Figure 1.2.) The

FIGURE 1.2

Number of U.S. Households with Net Worth of $10 Million or More, 1995–2000 (in millions)

(Compound Annual Growth Rate, 1995–2000 = 13.2%)

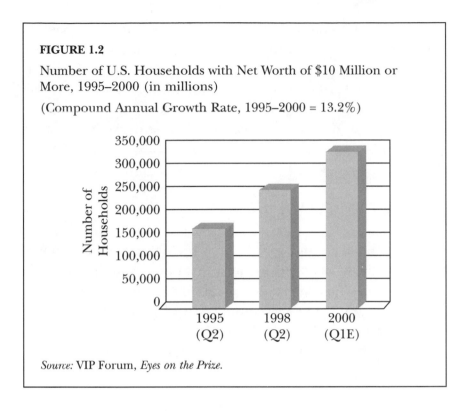

Source: VIP Forum, *Eyes on the Prize.*

VIP Forum, a Washington, D.C.–based research firm that tracks the wealthy, estimates that decamillionaires now account for 0.3 percent of all U.S. households.

Want an even more impressive statistic? The number of decamillionaire households where *liquid financial assets*—not just net worth—exceeds $10 million has grown by 17.4 percent on a compound annual basis since 1995. Today, almost 112,000 U.S. families are in this stratospheric subsegment (Bill Whitt, *Eyes on the Prize,* VIP Forum, 2000).

Whether one believes the concentration of wealth is a sign of capitalism's virtue, its vulgarity, or a completely benign by-product of its vigor, the fact remains: a narrow, yet extremely rich, layer of wealthy individuals constitutes the icing atop the nation's economic cake.

These five-million-plus wealthy families—encompassing America's semiaffluent, modestly affluent, affluent, and extremely affluent households—constitute a target market attracting thousands of stockbrokers, investment advisors, financial planners, accountants, and other financial intermediaries. The competition for the hearts and pocketbooks of these wealthy families is intense, and the winners on this platinum battleground will be the advisors who understand the needs of America's wealthy elite and deliver the services they demand.

THE ROUTE TO WEALTH

Before we understand what America's wealthiest families want in the way of financial advice, we must first understand how they became wealthy. Unlike previous generations, today's wealth is largely self-made, not inherited. According to *Forbes,* only 22 percent of the 400 wealthiest individuals in the United States in 1999 had inherited their wealth. In 1984, *Forbes* reported that 32 percent of the 400 were heirs.

Today, most wealth is in the hands of individuals who own private businesses. In fact, a recent Prince & Associates survey of the affluent found that 64 percent of high-net-worth investors are owners of a private business. Another 13 percent are professionals who acquired their wealth as a result of operating a private practice. Roughly 10 percent came into wealth as a result of investments, while inheritance was the source of just 7 percent of wealth of those surveyed. While the fabulous salaries and options of top corporate executives make headlines, those executives account for a small fraction of the wealthy.

In their bestseller, *The Millionaire Next Door,* Thomas J. Stanley and William D. Danko succinctly describe most of today's affluent: business owners and self-employed professionals. Excluding retirees, the authors say that more than two-thirds of affluent households are headed by self-employed business owners. The self-employed are four times more likely to be millionaires than those who work for others. The authors also debunk the myth that most of today's wealthy individuals are clones of Bill Gates. Sure, Silicon Valley start-ups and the much-publicized high-tech IPOs have created thousands of new millionaires. But affluent families are more likely to have made their money in dull, prosaic businesses such as dry cleaning, roofing maintenance, horse breeding, and janitorial contracting. Stanley and Danko's main point is that capital accumulation occurs largely among modest- to high-income business owners and self-employed professionals who maintain a frugal lifestyle. In short, the surgeon driving a brand-new Mercedes is less likely to be affluent than the guy driving a five-year-old Mercury whose company cleans the surgeon's waiting room.

The typical affluent customer of a financial services provider, therefore, is likely to be an independent businessperson or a self-employed professional.

Implications for the Financial Advisor

Relating your services to business owners requires an understanding of how they view their wealth and the path to achieving it. For most business owners, their business is their passion; it's their very life. Most businesses are small, private entities that may be worth very little to anyone except the business owner and his or her family. We estimate that the typical small business that creates an affluent client sells for $500,000 to $2 million. Most business owners built their businesses over many years. Don't forget, these businesses are, for the most part, the invisible dry cleaners, machine shops, and roofing companies that rarely attract attention, go public, or are based on a cutting-edge idea. They are businesses built on the owner's skillful management of assets and a careful eye on costs and liabilities. As a result, business owners view their income and wealth in financial statement form. They achieve profitability by increasing sales and managing expenses. Few business owners succeed based on sales alone, however; most are adept at managing the bottom line—which eventually comes to them.

Since business owners do not think in account-value terms, financial advisors concentrating on business owners should start to think like a small business owner. When you look at each of the business owner's assets, also look at the corresponding liability. For example, the business itself is an asset. But the business has no value unless the owner can find a buyer. That's why business succession planning is perennially a top concern among business owners. Advisors who can help guide their clients through the thicket of succession issues—which are as much psychological as they are financial—are highly esteemed.

Consider the business owner's other asset-liability concerns. For example, advisors typically emphasize their value in increasing the size of an investor's assets. But to the business owner, maximizing estate value through savvy asset management pales in importance to estate tax reduction. Any increase in wealth that a few more basis points of investment profit will bring to an estate is more than eradicated by an outdated estate plan, which can expose the business to huge tax liabilities and threaten its very existence.

Similarly, the disability of the business owner can threaten both the business and his or her personal and family wealth. Yet, depending on their background, many financial advisors ignore this risk. Stockbrokers and investment advisors mostly talk about assets and investments. While insurance professionals concentrate on liabilities and minimizing the risks of death, disability, and failing health, they usually neglect the asset side of the equation. Most affluent clients think about both sides of their balance sheet, as depicted below. They need help with the full picture of their wealth.

The Business Owner's Balance Sheet

Assets	*Liabilities*
Business	Succession
Estate	Estate taxes
Investments	Income and capital gains taxes
Liquidity	Disability
Retirement income	Long-term care costs

WHAT'S ON THEIR MINDS

Aside from planning for estates, taxes, and wealth, which business owners ranked as their top concern in a recent survey, what else do affluent business owners worry about? Their most common responses reflect understandable and down-to-earth issues.

Retirement planning. This is a complex issue. If your clients are like many we've spoken with, the preferred age for retirement is 55. Yet the prospects for such an early departure from the workplace have huge financial implications, especially if the clients are responsible for children who might still need assistance and parents who may require attention and financial support.

Asset protection. This refers to the general risks faced by business owners as a result of operating a business. A business owner may be seen by the unscrupulous or litigious as a deep-pocket target for lawsuits or fraud. Private practice physicians, for example, often lament the high cost of malpractice insurance, but can't operate without it. Similarly, construction firms face risks in the form of environmental law violations or on-the-job accidents where employees are hurt or property is damaged. Fines and lawsuits can devastate a small business that is not adequately insured.

Disability income protection. Since the greatest asset of any small business is usually the business owner, disability income protection is vital. Any accident or illness that impairs the owner's ability to devote full-time attention to the business strikes a serious blow.

Success of children. Perhaps to the surprise of the less well off, wealthy business owners worry about the success of their children. They want their offspring to grow up to be responsible and independent adults, comfortable with money but not spoiled by it. They wonder whether their adult children will return home after college or their first jobs for financial or psychological reasons. As the *New York Times* recently reported, this "boomerang" factor is of concern to the affluent—and should be to their advisors.

Health care. This is a concern of all clients, and affluent business owners are no different. We'll discuss this issue in greater detail later, but keep in mind the vulnerability felt by business owners who want to be prepared for contingencies. As an advisor, you have the opportunity to help them address and overcome their health care fears.

Elder care. Care of elderly parents and relatives is another ticking time bomb among affluent clients. Currently, about one-quarter of U.S. families provide care for an elderly relative or friend. Increased longevity, fueled by advances in health care and living standards, is creating a population boom among the elderly that will increase as baby boomers age. The issue for current clients is not so much the cost of providing for their own care, but rather the possibility that they may have to fund elder care for their parents or other relatives. This possibility, plus the potential for having to provide the actual physical care elderly relatives or other loved ones may need, could compromise your clients' plans for their own golden years. Even affluent clients worry about these elder care demands, since they are an unquantifiable unknown and have the potential to be enormously expensive and demanding.

Charitable giving. As stock prices surged over recent years, charitable giving increased. This greater generosity reflects an interest in sharing with the greater community and "giving back."

WHAT'S IN THEIR MINDS

The affluent business owner has a different mindset from the affluent client who has inherited wealth or the executive who made it to the top by climbing the corporate ladder and earning stock options. The business owner is predisposed to investing in the business first because the risks are known. Business owners don't consider such investments too risky or an "overconcentration in one asset class," to use a term a financial planner might prefer. In fact, many business owners look skeptically at the stock market as being too risky. As one client asked Steve, "Why would I trade investment in my own business, where I know the payoff, for the uncertainty of ownership in a company I don't know and where I am just one of a zillion faceless shareholders?"

One advisor we know in Pittsburgh throws up his hands when his clients—many of them successful real estate investors and developers—say that it's a better time to invest in real estate than in the stock market. "What do you do about that?" he laments. Real estate has great appeal for the affluent because it offers a tangible store of wealth with both inflation protection and potential tax benefits through the deductibility of mortgage interest, depreciation, and other expenses. (Remember how easy it was to interest affluent clients in real estate limited partnerships in the early 1980s?) Managed correctly, real estate can be the ideal investment for wealthy clients. In fact, real estate is the most common business interest of the affluent in the United States, and real estate agents and developers represent about 15 percent of the affluent business owners in the nation. Moreover, the popularity of real estate investing among the wealthy confirms their balance sheet view of things: a piece of property is an asset that produces income, which is offset by a mortgage liability and expenses. This balance sheet way of thinking is an approach you might adopt when relating to the affluent.

Other ways of managing and perceiving risk are unique to the small business mindset, too. The "business owner barbell" is a way many affluent clients try to balance investment risk. A business owner may anchor one end of his holdings with extremely risky vehicles such as private equity and venture capital, then use extremely safe and liquid short-term municipal bonds at the other end. Absent entirely from this mixture of extreme risk and extreme security is an investment in moderately risky securities like quality stocks. "Anyone can invest in stocks" is a phrase we've heard from many affluent barbell investors. Where venture capital and private equity may seem risky to "ordinary" investors, small business owners feel comfortable assessing the risks of these vehicles, probably because they encounter similar risks in their own businesses. They find comfort, as well, in the liquidity of short-term instruments. When Steve was a brokerage firm executive in the 1980s, he saw many Keogh plans owned by affluent physicians and other professionals where the holdings were 100 percent fixed income. In some cases, these tax-advantaged plans even owned tax-free municipal bonds! So security conscious were these business owners that they paid for tax benefits they didn't use.

Winning Tactic

Affluent business owners don't invest to get rich—they already have money.

Talking to them about investing is almost irrelevant if you have not first proven your desire and ability to help them protect their existing wealth against possible loss.

First build the moat. Then build the castle.

Business Owners as Indicators

The stock market is one of the most reliable leading indicators of the economy. In the midst of recession, stock prices begin to climb, heralding the start of an economic recovery. Similarly, when the economy is booming, a drop in stock prices often signals a business slowdown just over the horizon. In early 2001, evidence of such a business decline was taking shape.

The Nasdaq's terrible 2000 performance may have indicated that the real economy was about to suffer; meetings we've held with advisors from Seattle to New York have revealed a growing concern among their business-owner clients. While business owners are generally an optimistic lot, so much of their psychic and financial investments are tied to their businesses that any threat to these ventures can shake their confidence. For advisors, a drop in their client's sales, a dip in profits, or a decline in confidence often translates into a reluctance on the part of the business owner to withdraw funds from his business and invest those funds with you.

You can prove your value to your business-owner clients by talking to them about their business, about the markets they serve, and their prospects for the near term. Be focused and take the time to truly understand their challenges. One affluent business owner told Steve, "The biggest frustration I have as a business owner is that there is no one I can talk to about my challenges. It's not fair to talk so candidly with employees—and it would scare my family." By taking an active interest in your client's business, you can fill that important void.

WHAT'S IN THEIR HEARTS

As much as they are concerned about business success and wealth, the bottom line for most affluent business owners is family. In our discussions with affluent investors and their advisors, we found that the affluent most often consider their families as the principal beneficiaries of their wealth. A recent Prince & Associates research project for *Institutional Investor* confirmed that the largest single group of high-net-worth clients—nearly 21 percent—says that investing for the family is their most important goal. This paternalism results in a desire to engage in estate planning, retirement planning, and other efforts to preserve and expand capital to take care of the affluent family's future needs. Ironically, despite this strong desire to protect their families, we estimate that fewer than 25 percent of affluent clients have a current estate plan!

Let's take a closer look at what the heads of these affluent households want for their families. In fact, let's first sit in on a real sales call with the head of an affluent household and see why this call, which started with so much promise, ultimately fizzled.

The Call

A broker/consultant at a leading wirehouse arranged a meeting with Steve and the CEO of a large, publicly held technology company in Silicon Valley. The CEO was a self-made success, building his firm from scratch in the early days of microchips. He endured many painful setbacks along the way, but climbed out of them. The broker was excited about the possibility of working with such a prestigious client.

The meeting started with cordial greetings and a brief discussion of the company, its history, and the CEO's current interest in retaining an investment management consultant and the services of one or more asset management companies. The broker, the CEO, and Steve seemed to be getting along well, and the broker was visibly pleased and confident.

The trouble began when the broker took his turn to speak. He began to describe his favorite investment managers. He explained how many of his top managers were aggressive investors who took positions in small-capitalization and emerging-growth companies. These managers took great risks and often reaped even greater returns. Rather than being pleased, the CEO turned grim. Steve got worried. The broker, not understanding his prospect's growing concern, became more animated and attempted to draw the CEO closer to the managers by suggesting they sought the same type of growth that he had created. The CEO cut him off.

"That's precisely what I *don't* want," he sputtered. "My family has endured enough risk for one lifetime." The broker was speechless.

What went wrong? The high-tech CEO was being completely open and honest. He sincerely wanted to find a trustworthy consultant and professional asset manager to handle a family trust he'd created for the benefit of his children and grandchildren. He didn't have time to take an active role in the management of the money, nor did he have the expertise to develop an investment process that would generate both growth of capital and consistent income. He also realized that his current personal investments were very high risk. Not only was much of his wealth tied to the volatile stock of his company; he also participated in several venture capital and private equity deals. Like many successful entrepreneurs, he had invested only in areas he understood.

The broker-consultant's error was coming into the meeting ignorant of *why* the CEO was investing. The broker assumed the CEO was investing his own money for his own benefit and that his investment philosophy would reflect his tolerance for business risk. In most instances, that's a faulty assumption. In most cases, the affluent are investing on behalf of their family.

What "Family" Means

Investing for the benefit of family or to ensure continued financial independence so they won't be a burden to family members are the true "big picture" issues. One client's view of family needs and how to provide for them may be very different from the outlook and choices of another client. That's why in-depth personal discussions between prospective client and advisor are necessary before any suggestions can be made. In general, however, the array of family issues with which wealthy investors and their advisors must deal are remarkably similar from investor to investor.

Protect their spouse. While women entrepreneurs and professionals are growing in number and will become a major force in the near future, most self-employed affluent entrepreneurs at present are men. For them, taking care of family means, in part, ensuring that their wives are protected. This general need translates into specific services including estate planning, the execution of wills and trusts, and creating various forms of income protection.

Assist their children. Invariably the cost of a child's education is an expense wealthy individuals want to make sure they cover. They also often want to provide funds, in whole or in part, for their children to purchase a home, start a business, get specialized training, or help with any special health or emotional need. Wealthy individuals also may want to provide for the education of their grandchildren.

Assist their parents. Wealthy individuals may wish to assume, in whole or in part, the costs of housing, health care, and other expenses of their aging parents. These other expenses may include the purchase or maintenance of a retirement home, travel, in-home attendants, nurses, physical therapists, companions, or nursing home care.

Provide for an independent retirement. Not only does this involve setting up individual and corporate retirement accounts, it also means investigating long-term health care insurance, disability insurance, real estate needs, and, of course, investment planning.

Prepare for trouble-free disengagement from the business. Since a business is often the wealth-creation machine of an affluent household, planning for the end game of the family's involvement in the business is generally of great concern. Whether a decision is made to sell the business, arrange for younger family members take it over, or liquidate it, the affluent household requires help in planning and understanding the legal and tax consequences of their choices.

Provide for the broader community. Wealthy individuals often are interested in the needs of those beyond their own immediate families. Because many want to give back something to the larger family of man, charitable considerations often take on great meaning. Advisors who ask meaningful questions in this area when discussing estate planning may be surprised by what they discover. Sometimes, wealthy clients and prospects may not have identified or articulated this desire.

What's the Money For?

Not long ago, Steve was invited to give a talk at the firm that employs Keith G., a prominent authority on charitable giving. An advisor who was not an attorney and did not understand estate strategies was meeting with an oil company executive who had just elected to retire early. The advisor asked Keith to come to the meeting and, since Steve was in town, he was invited to tag along.

Most of the lunch discussion focused on estate planning alternatives for the executive who, like many successful businesspeople, did not have a current estate plan in place. The executive listened patiently and asked questions. Then Steve, aware the executive had no immediate family, asked what the money was for. The client seemed startled at first, but encouraged to proceed, he began to discuss his wealth.

He explained that since he had no family who needed his estate, he had not really thought about the beneficiaries of his will. Asked again about the things that were important to him and what he might do to change the world, he began to reveal his long-standing dislike of his industry's impact on the environment and his nagging guilt about injured animals. He had several pets of his own and had written checks to a nearby animal shelter, as well as to national organizations. He then gave an animated lecture about the best ways to combat industrial environmental damage and preserve wildlife.

"I'm glad you asked me what the money was for," the executive said at the end of lunch, "no one ever asked me that question. I really hadn't thought about it before." But as a result of the question, the executive gave his advisor a $2 million investment management account. Ironically, the executive was weighing another advisor's estate planning suggestions at the time of the lunch. The meeting, in fact, was sort of a "last chance" before following the path suggested by the competitor. Our advisor had no idea he was so vulnerable.

HIDDEN CONCERNS

Aside from family-related issues, wealthy business owners have other wants and desires. Many times these are not discussed with advisors—largely because advisors don't ask and may not seem to care. Here are some of the wants and desires affluent business owners have expressed to attentive advisors. As you can see, few of these deep desires have anything to do with investing; in fact, because the affluent businesspeople have the resources, often money is not a direct part of their wishes.

A fulfilling retirement. The boom in 20- and 30-something high-tech millionaires has helped reshape the traditional view of retirement. The "R" word no longer means working until age 65 and moving to a retirement community. More business owners are trading a retirement of leisure for second careers, new start-ups, and new combinations of work and leisure. What will the new retirees do? Where will they live? How will their financial needs change? Many financial advisors have not considered these changes and are currently being caught off guard. Will you be a valued counselor and assist them in their dreams, or will you sit back with their doubters and watch?

A sympathetic, knowledgeable ear. Many of your clients have incomplete thoughts about their future and need help developing a plan. They're frustrated because they have trouble finding a sympathetic sounding board free of some conflict of interest. Business associates, for example, would be concerned about the impact of any decision on them. Accountants and attorneys can offer advice, but their counsel may reflect their status as advisors to the current business state of affairs. Any new ideas could be threatening, and besides, who wants to ruminate about the future when the meter is running at $400 per hour? Even family members, who should provide unqualified support, often are content with the status quo and may resent any change. A trusted financial advisor may be the perfect listener.

A desire to travel. Many affluent clients have been so busy building businesses they may have sacrificed free time and avoided vacations. The sales manager of a major wirehouse tapped into this opportunity to help his affluent clients and generate additional business. He and his colleagues polled their affluent clients for locations the clients had considered but never visited. One of the most popular locales was Asia. He then worked with an outstanding travel agent to create a custom tour of Asia that would cover sites and cultural activities overlooked by big tour operators. The agent provided materials and refreshments at a meeting to which clients were invited, many of whom brought along friends. The meeting was a success and the branch plans additional sessions.

A desire to maximize their time. Many successful clients are so busy they delegate many tasks most people do themselves. Often, to maximize money-making time, clients will delegate opening the mail, making travel reservations, scheduling meetings, as well as matters that involve law, accounting, and investing. What about other tasks? One advisor noticed that his client was so busy that, as a favor, he offered to help negotiate a new car deal and complete the paperwork. He was surprised at the client's look of relief when he made the offer. The transaction went off without a hitch and the client was delighted. Then the big surprise occurred: the advisor got a call the next week from a local entrepreneur seek-

ing a meeting to discuss investments. The caller was a friend of the
car buyer and was impressed by the advisor's level of service!

Fear of abandonment. The wives of affluent businessmen face
their own unique worry—what would happen to them in the event
of widowhood or divorce? Even clients who believe their relationships are solid think about this issue, and some may have contem-
plated leaving their marriage and wondered what their share of the
assets might be. One banker, with the help of an attorney special-
izing in matrimonial law, began holding a series of workshops
about finance for affluent women. The key topic was a "postnup-
tial" agreement that states the terms of asset partitioning among a
couple in the event of divorce. The banker was astounded by the
referrals every seminar produced.

A not-so-obvious—but real—abandonment fear concerns the
loss of you as your client's advisor. Chuck R., a successful advisor in
Raleigh, North Carolina, learned this firsthand. After faithfully serving an older couple for many years, Chuck thought he knew everything about them. When the husband died, Chuck called to offer
his help to the widow. He was shocked when she told him that a
well-known trust company would be caring for her assets. Still want-
ing to be supportive to his longtime client and friend, Chuck in-
quired of the widow why she had chosen the bank. On the verge of
tears, she told Chuck that the choice had absolutely nothing to do
with him or the quality of his services. The decision, in fact, hadn't
been hers. In the estate plan completed by her husband, a plan
Chuck knew about, the trust company was named successor trustee.

"My husband was afraid something might happen to you, Chuck,
and he wanted to make sure I would be cared for," the widow told
him sadly. Chuck lost out on the opportunity to meet the ongoing
financial needs of a client simply because the client did not realize
that the advisor was more than a one-man band and was afraid that
his wife would be abandoned if something happened to him. How
many of your clients are concerned about something happening to
you? Research of affluent business owners indicates that their primary financial concerns are for estate planning and business suc-

cession. If their most pressing issues are for their own succession, why would they jeopardize the financial security of their families by trusting an advisor who leaves them exposed by not discussing his own succession plans?

Do You Know Your Clients?

To uncover the innermost hopes and fears of your clients, try this exercise. Look at the list below, and fill in the blanks for your top three clients only. If there are any categories where responses are missing, go back to your clients and start getting the answers.

Favorite investment topic they like to discuss _____

_____

Favorite vacation places _____

Passions (art, sports, collections) _____

Favorite charity(ies) _____

Retirement dream and location _____

_____

Special demands (caregiver to elderly, disabled child) _____

_____

Keep tabs on the answers because they will change. Add these information fields to your contact management software and use the information as a reminder to discuss the topics often with your top clients. Drop each a note or send an article when you see information on a subject they enjoy, and send an appropriate book from time to time. This interest shows your genuine concern for your clients as people, not as accounts.

OPENING THE BUSINESS OWNER'S DOOR

Your biggest challenge over the next few years will be to demonstrate that you care about your clients. As we're going to see, the competition is heating up, and if your clients don't believe you know and care about them as people—not just as consumers of your investment, insurance, and banking products—you may lose them.

If the key to a man's heart is through his stomach, the key to a business owner's wallet is through the business. Here are a few ways to open the door.

- *Focus on the business.* The owner's passion is the business—not the stock market. Get to know it before you make any attempt to contact the owner. Gather information. Sometimes the best way to do that is simply to walk around the property, talk to customers, or become a customer yourself.
- *Ask questions about the business.* In addition to gathering information, be prepared to ask knowledgeable questions: "Why do you offer service X but your competitor doesn't?" "Why do you emphasize Y in your promotions?" The questions show your genuine interest and prompt the owner to think about business essentials.
- *Stick to a few basic services.* Alternative financing, retirement plans, and cash management remain the Big Three. What do you have that's better than what the business owner currently uses? Remember, making money through investing is not business owners' primary concern—saving money or time, improving returns on cash, and simplifying their lives are what's important.

- *Write a short note to set up an appointment.* Here's the gist of such a note: "Dear Ms. Smith—I've watched the growth of Smith Co. for several years and have noted with particular interest your ability to expand in a very competitive environment. I'd very much like to learn more about your company and see how we at Financial Co. can assist you. We have developed several services for businesses like yours, including programs to maximize yield on corporate cash, as well as many innovative retirement plans and financing options. I'd like to see if there is a fit and will call for an appointment."
- *Call personally.* Call at 7 AM and you'll have the best chance to get past a protective secretary or switchboard.
- *When in doubt, ask about the business.* Let the owner tell you how the business started and how it is run—and let him talk until he drops.
- *Warning.* Not all businesses are successes. Investigate before you start your efforts.

QUESTIONS TO ASK YOUR CLIENTS

Once you break the ice and demonstrate that you genuinely care, clients often are extremely willing to tell you what's in their minds and hearts. When the time is right—at a good point in a conversation when you know you have established rapport—ask some of the following questions in a way that is most comfortable for you:

- When you envision the future, in what activities do you see yourself engaged?
- What worries you most about the future as far as your loved ones are concerned?
- What specific future events concern you the most (for example, paying for a child's wedding, buying a retirement home, taking care of aged parents, being confined to a nursing home, paying for a grandchild's education, business succession)?

- With whom in your family do you speak freely about money?
- Would you rather live more modestly and leave a big estate or spend what you like to satisfy your needs and leave a smaller estate?
- What worries you most about being alone?

Client Meeting Action Checklist

Before your next meeting with a client, make sure you understand:

1. The purposes for which the client's capital ultimately will be used

   - Retirement
   - Travel
   - Children's education
   - Grandchildren's education
   - Assistance to parents
   - Business buyout
   - Charitable contributions

2. For whom your client is investing

   - Spouse
   - Children
   - Parents
   - Favorite charity

3. The broad range of your client's emotions and what they mean in specific terms

   - Fears
   - Hopes
   - Passions
   - Dreams

Chapter 2

*I*nvestment Advisor or Wealth Advisor?

| *One role will shrink, the other grow.*

Are you an investment advisor or a wealth advisor? Do your clients look to you for stocks and investment ideas or do they consider you a trusted colleague qualified to assist them with all their financial concerns?

If most of your income currently comes from commissions and most of your clients think of you as the person who delivers product ideas, you are still in the investment advisor camp. If you are like many transaction-oriented advisors, the bull market probably has been kind to you, and there is little pressing incentive to do something different. But times are changing. While many of your peers will continue to prosper as stock pickers and product salespersons, this segment will shrink. The challenge facing most financial professionals is whether to become more expert in a particular product or service area or to make the transition to the wider role of wealth manager.

Specialist versus Generalist:
A Tale of Two Models

Success in serving the affluent market comes in many forms. Let's look at two examples that illustrate how an in-depth product specialty and a wealth management focus can both be winning formulas.

Dennis M. is an investment advisor at a wirehouse branch in Boston. He and his partner specialize in private equity investments, selling hundreds of millions of dollars' worth of private equity deals to wealthy investors. They track managers, partnerships, and distributions. They know which deals are pending and which are making payments. They truly are specialists and experts in private equity. On the client side, they maintain a detailed database of private equity investors and actively serve their clients. When other advisors or friends of clients want to know anything about private equity, they come to Dennis and his partner. Should they become wealth generalists? No!

Private equity is an area with which Dick Thalheimer probably has only passing familiarity. Dick heads a five-person advisor team at the New England Guild in Boston. The principals of the firm all are in second careers after having had success as corporate executives in the financial services industry. Thalheimer and his team use a process they call "Context Sensitive Investment Management," which allows them to understand a client's high-level strategic goals and the forces that are driving them. The process doesn't focus on specific products, but looks at issues such as estate planning, retirement planning, taxes, and emotional concerns. More than anything else, the team gets to know the clients and develops a sense of trust. The team has developed deep relationships with many business owners in its region and has developed a thriving practice. Should it dig deeper into a product area and become more specialized? No!

THE CHANGING NATURE OF THE BUSINESS

Because of the changing nature of the financial services business and the growing wealth of the affluent market segment, today's brokers, planners, and advisors are called on to deal with the complex financial needs of their clients. Often, these needs go beyond investments. Whether clients are currently aware of their major life needs or even looking for a solution, they need help with major life and business issues. They want to provide for their families if they die or become disabled, and reduce the bite of taxes, particularly on their estates. They want to realize the value of their small business and pass it along to a viable successor; and they want to protect themselves from lawsuits in an increasingly litigious society.

These needs create demand for advisors who can see the big picture and provide comprehensive answers and solutions. As a result of history and the regulatory demarcation of banking, insurance, and securities, this comprehensive way of viewing customer needs is still rather new. But the demand is there. In the past, providing investment advice, or loans, or insurance products was enough. Today, these are components of a solution, not the solution itself. For financial professionals who come from the securities industry, this presents a quandary.

Providing investment advice and products was, and continues to be, profitable. But will it continue to be and will investment advice remain a viable service? Yes, but with a caveat: Advice and the advice giver must become more specialized. With information more readily available to the general public, there is great value in knowing one area particularly well. For example, experts in areas as diverse as municipal bonds, options, restricted stock transactions, and closed-end funds find their practices booming. In fact, as more brokers and planners set up team and group practices and seek to develop reputations for expertise, this type of specialization will become even more desirable.

Unfortunately, the core skill set and favorite activity for many advisors—stock picking—will become a more difficult base on which to build a business. Performance is the chief yardstick of stock picking, and superior performance will be more difficult to achieve on a consistent basis in the future.

Market volatility. Bull markets support the stock picker. When the public is convinced equity values can only rise, they assume someone monitoring the market for a living can determine which stocks will be outstanding performers. But when markets fall, as they have recently, confidence in stock picking is damaged. When a dot-com stock outperforms the Dow by 300 percent then collapses without warning, clients wonder about the value of "professional" advice.

The explosion of financial information. At one time, the newspaper financial pages and the *Wall Street Journal* were read by a limited segment of the public. Today, newspapers and personal finance magazines are widely read, and vie for attention with personal finance Web sites and—perhaps the most influential medium of all—television. Nonstop financial news and the availability of virtually limitless financial data may not help investors make better decisions, but it reminds them unceasingly of performance and acquaints them with some of the most notable—and most glib—celebrities in the investment world. Your what-have-you-done-for-me-lately clients may wonder: If you're such a great stock picker, how come you're not on TV?

The boom in indexing. While not every investor is familiar with Modern Portfolio Theory and efficient markets, many have come to the conclusion that, over time, they can't beat the market—even with your help. The growth of low-cost index funds and the widespread implementation of asset allocation principles in portfolio construction demonstrate this fact. Fewer individuals than in the past believe that they or their advisors can really pick consistent winners. While they might use a stock-picking broker for a small portion of their portfolio, such a broker won't get their serious money.

The growth of online brokerage. For those who approach the stock market as a form of entertainment or gambling (although investors who share that view probably would never admit it, even to themselves), online brokerage offers many advantages over a human broker or advisor. It's faster, cheaper, and more discreet. And while the investor can't blame a stockbroker for poor choices, why pass up the thrill of acting immediately on a hunch, something heard over CNBC, or on research available online? The truth of the matter: Investors who buy and sell online probably do no better or worse than those who trade to the same degree using a human intermediary. Of course, a human broker would probably advise a client not to trade so much or to be much more selective in his or her choices. But many stock pickers have a propensity to trade, and since there are no published results for the stock-picking ability of retail brokers, no one knows how well or how poorly they perform. Many investors who have been disappointed by broker performance in the past have found they can do at least as well themselves, and at less cost.

The fickleness of customers. Over the years, research has found that few affluent clients put all their financial eggs in one basket. Most wealthy clients—about three-quarters, according to some estimates—deal with more than one advisor and institution. In fact, it's not uncommon for a wealthy investor to have three or more advisors. At a recent meeting of the Securities Industry Association for retail sales managers, for instance, Evan observed a panel of wealthy investors who described how they would add and delete advisors based on the level of performance. Unless they were extremely satisfied with the service and returns they received from an advisor, the affluent investors would readily add a new advisor to their stable—and just as readily cut the advisor whose performance had slipped.

The growth of the professionally managed account industry. Today's stock-picking brokers are not just competing against the wirehouse or regional firm broker down the street. Tens of thousands of professional managers at mutual funds, hedge funds, and other money management organizations are making investment decisions each day. Informed clients know this and are skeptical of the ability of an individual broker or advisor to consistently outperform market professionals. Less informed clients may be willing to give a broker or advisor a shot—until performance fails to meet some arbitrary and often unrealistic goal. The enormous growth of separately managed accounts is evidence of the success of professionally managed money. These accounts' popularity—a testament to the broker's waning ability to compete with professional money managers—is a profitable, successful, and astute way of admitting that "if you can't beat 'em, join 'em."

The Problem with Performance . . .

*A*ffluent clients consider "performance" to be the most important factor in choosing an investment advisor. And why shouldn't it be? After all, what other objective measure can be used to differentiate one advisor from another in a sea of providers when the service the client is being sold is an investment?

Banks, brokerages, insurance companies, and financial planning firms all offer minor variations of the same investment products. Whether the need is stocks, mutual funds, or investment-related insurance, most providers can meet the demand with products that are virtual commodities.

What about substantive differences in the advisors themselves (that is, distinctions not based on personality or style)? Titles have nothing to do with the quality of advice and, if anything, add to the confusion. Today's providers have titles that are reminiscent of DNA molecules: Rearrange the words *financial, advisor, consultant, investment,* and *representative* and the permutations yield the titles of financial providers at virtually every firm in America. Since there is no Morningstar or Zagat's to rate advisors, who can tell how good they are? Absent any other measure when selecting an advisor for stock-picking ability, clients are almost forced to turn to performance as a measuring tool.

. . . And the Hidden Benefit of Separately Managed Accounts

The growth of managed accounts diffuses the performance issue and adds an element to service that often has been missing: consistency. Variation of service is a multi-million-dollar problem at securities firms, which they try to address through training, automation, compliance, and supervision. The essence of the issue is this: A wide variety of advisors work at national, regional, local, and independent securities firms. They employ highly consultative, sophisticated wealth managers, as well as transactional, cold-calling cowboys. They employ advisors who know every detail of certain products, and those who shun the same products. They employ advisors who embrace financial planning as an essential, ongoing process, and those who grudgingly enter numbers into the software when a client asks for a formal plan. In short, the level of service a customer can expect to receive from any one firm varies widely.

Imagine the affluent client's perception of a typical firm. Whether it's a wirehouse spending hundreds of millions of dollars on national advertising or a local firm working hard in its area to establish a favorable image, the aim is the same: to convince a prospect that a qualified investment professional is available through the firm's doors. Yet who is the prospect likely to encounter? A professional? Or will the prospect be handed over to a salesperson?

What results among affluent investors, then, is an almost schizoid view of Wall Street. Some clients at the large firms consider their Merrill, Salomon, or PaineWebber advisor to be their financial guru, and the firms to be powerhouses of investment banking, research, and asset management. Other investors—at the very same firms, but served by different advisors—see Wall Street as one big sales machine, seeking to enrich itself by pushing any and every possible product through a sales force that the firms now, in this view at least, euphemistically have renamed *financial advisors*. The differences among advisors at smaller firms tend to be not as great because the cultures tend to be more homogeneous, but they are not immune to the problem.

Separately managed accounts have added a welcome measure of consistency to service delivery at securities firms by separating a product and its performance aspects from the person who delivers it. By institutionalizing the product, a firm knows that the portfolio of a client in Pittsburgh and the portfolio of a client in Pasadena will receive virtually the same level of attention and service. Sure, the personalities of the advisors handling the clients in those cities will differ, but even in the area of one-on-one client contact, the firm can set standards and establish guidelines. The burden of performance is lifted from the shoulders of the advisor to those of the portfolio manager. And when the manager's performance suffers, he or she can be dumped—not the securities firm or the advisor.

MOVING TOWARD WEALTH MANAGEMENT

If you asked the head of an affluent family whether he or she is in the market for wealth management services, you'd probably get a blank look. The affluent rarely ask for such services directly because few think in those terms or know that providers exist. Nevertheless, help in managing their wealth is what they want. And when they get the help, they're willing to pay for it like they pay for any other service—through a fee. In survey after survey, both by providers of services and by independent research firms, affluent clients overwhelmingly say they prefer flat or asset-based fees to commissions when buying financial services.

The numbers bear out this preference: Fee-based advisors were the fastest growing group in terms of client asset accumulation during the 1994–1998 period, according to Tiburon Strategic Advisors. They grew at a faster rate than discount brokers, mutual fund companies, full-service brokers, and banks. Separately managed accounts—those sold through brokers and advisors, and managed by professional money managers—also have grown at a rapid pace. Total assets in managed accounts stood at $163 billion in 1996, $230 billion in 1997, and $328 billion in 1998. Assets reached $425 billion at year-end 1999, according to the Money Management Institute (MMI). And the numbers continue to grow, reflecting a desire for both professional money management and fee-based payment. Investors who have become accustomed to investing in mutual funds often find investing in managed accounts the logical next step.

Interestingly, this type of investing is growing in popularity at the home of traditional stockbrokers—the largest Wall Street firms. At the end of the third quarter of 2000, assets under management at Merrill Lynch, Morgan Stanley Dean Witter, PaineWebber, Prudential, and Salomon Smith Barney stood at $315 billion, or about two-thirds of total managed account assets industry-wide. At medium and small firms surveyed by the MMI—including Brinker Capital, Lockwood Financial, PMC, Trust Company of America, and Wells Fargo—growth is increasing as well. Assets under management at these and similar firms grew from $35 billion at year-end 1997 to $56 billion at the end of 1998 to almost $88 billion at year-end 1999.

The Historic Allure of Managed Accounts

*T*he recent popularity of separately managed accounts often is attributed to market volatility and the growing awareness that the accounts offer tax advantages over mutual funds. But this is not the first wave of interest in the product.

E.F. Hutton pioneered separately managed accounts in 1973. The pioneers were industry veterans John Ellis, Jim Lockwood, and Dick Schilffarth, and later Len Reinhart and Frank Campanale. The 1987 crash and its aftermath spurred another round of growth. Hutton dropped account minimums to $100,000, and Merrill Lynch, Advest, and Wheat First soon followed. Clients and brokers alike were seeking refuge from self-directed accounts, and were attracted to the professionally managed process that included a true investment policy statement, due diligence of professional managers, and a periodic review of investment performance.

Watching clients head for the exits after the 1987 crash, Steve and Advest Bank President John Beckert conducted a survey of $100,000-plus clients to understand why they were leaving. When asked in which product they most wanted to invest, the leading answer was "portfolio management." As those kinds of responses began to be heard throughout the industry, brokerage firm management began to deliver the first round of fee-based accounts.

Another wave of interest in separately managed accounts crested in 1997. That time, the victim was the online brokerage industry. Self-directed clients using the new medium got their first dose of humility when the Dow Jones Index suddenly dropped 554 points. Many large clients pulled their accounts from Schwab and Fidelity. Quick to respond to the loss of such important customers, Schwab redoubled its efforts to support the advisory side of its business, under the direction of John Coghlan. It introduced the Schwab Managed Account Connection, a platform of separately managed accounts, and later lured Jeff Cusack of Salomon Smith Barney to run the unit.

THE GROWING COMPETITIVE THREAT

In addition to meeting the diverse needs of their clients, more advisors are transitioning to wealth management because they recognize that other players are entering their space. Competition is heating up, and if you don't start providing the services your clients need, someone else will. Who are these new players?

Accountants

The American Institute of Certified Public Accountants estimates that more than 65,000 of the nation's 450,000 CPAs will enter the asset management or financial planning business over the next five years. Because of the high trust the CPA designation imparts, accountants have the potential to become formidable competitors in the wealth management arena. Already, at least 42 states permit accountants to receive commissions for investment sales. Supported by product companies anxious to expand distribution, a majority of accountants now plan to offer investment management services of some kind. Most accountants now say they are very interested in actually managing their clients' assets, not just providing financial advice or financial planning.

Brokerage firms already are working out formal referral programs for accountants, but for those seeking their own investment practice, brokerages H.D. Vest and First Global provide complete broker-dealer services. And while these firms already have over 10,000 advisors with securities and/or investment advisory licenses, their development is still in its early stages.

The AICPA reports that 3,000 accountants have been awarded its Personal Financial Planning Specialist (PFS) designation, double the number of 1977. More than 6,000 CPAs have earned the Certi-fied Financial Planner (CFP) designation—constituting more than 15 percent of total CFP licensees. And about 1,200 CPAs hold both PFS and CFP designations.

Phyllis Bernstein, director of the AICPA's Personal Financial Planning Division, says accountability for investment performance is the major stumbling block that prevents accountants from ex-panding into a broader wealth management role. Many CPAs fear that a quarter or two of poor returns would lead clients to jettison them as wealth managers, as well as dump them as their tax advisor and auditor. That's why, she explains, accountants venturing into wealth management typically outsource investing functions to third-party money managers. That way, the accountants can perform the monitoring and education roles for which they are esteemed.

This Accountant Means Business

*H*is views certainly aren't unbiased, but Stephen "Tony" Batman believes that accountants soon will dominate the delivery of financial services. An accountant by training him-self, Batman cofounded and heads 1st Global, Inc., a Dallas-based financial services firm that serves as the broker-dealer for more than 1,600 CPAs at 850 accounting firms.

"Accountants will become increasingly competitive be-cause of the incredible strength of the accounting brand," he says. "The public sees accountants as being credible, knowledgeable, and trustworthy, and looking out for the client's interests only—which are very important competitive differentiators."

What about the accountants' reputation for being poor communicators? "They're learning," says Batman, who adds that communications and selling skills are acquirable if a CPA is committed to the business. Batman says, through his firm accountants are compensated in a variety of ways for their insurance, brokerage, asset management, retirement planning, and estate planning work. They can be paid a flat annual retainer, hourly or per diem fees like paying for tax advice, disclosed commissions, or through a fee based on assets under management.

"The biggest myth perpetuated on the American public is that securities products are too difficult to understand or explain. Accountants can understand and explain them very well, and they don't come across with any hard-close sales techniques or talk anyone into doing anything that is inappropriate for them. They don't know it yet, but in five or ten years, most stockbrokers will be out of business. The fact of the matter is, people don't want financial services—they want their problems solved. And that's what accounting firms are great at."

If you still think accountants don't "get it," think again. Steve recently visited a wirehouse branch office in the Midwest where the branch manager and his team discussed the rise of nontraditional competitors. The branch manager was stressing the intensity of the competition, particularly since a local CPA firm recently had contracted with a provider of private-label managed account services and had begun to offer the accounts.

When one broker scoffed at the seriousness of the threat, the manager quickly served up the punch line: The CPA firm already had captured $50 million in assets from that branch alone!

Insurance Agents

At present, about three-quarters of life insurance agents provide estate and retirement planning. If these financial intermediaries overcome their own bias, which is a tendency to view an insurance policy as the solution to almost every financial problem, they will become effective competitors of those who come to wealth management from securities. Already, life agents have made inroads through the sales of variable annuities and mutual funds, and the sales arms of the full-line insurers are eager to expand the reach of their agents into additional securities products. Insurance agents have the ability to address many key concerns of affluent business owners: the risk of disability and the risk of lost income.

This latter risk is the precise concern targeted successfully by Northwestern Mutual Life Insurance agents. Aiming at private practice physicians and other self-employed professionals, Northwestern Mutual agents establish themselves early with clients who one day will have more money to invest. Northwestern has begun to leverage these relationships by buying a brokerage firm, Robert W. Baird, and an asset allocation and investment management firm, The Frank Russell Trust Company. One 35-year veteran agent confided that the securities and asset allocation services are comparatively easy to sell, compared to disability insurance. And because he does not manage the money himself, he says his clients consider his advice to be impartial and of great value.

Trust Companies

Traditionally targeting the extremely wealthy who inherited their assets, trust companies have become more aggressive marketers of late. Northern Trust is expanding beyond its Midwest base, while Harris Trust is seeking successful entrepreneurs. Schwab, of course, bought U.S. Trust and will likely expand its marketing efforts. In addition to the giants, many small, privately held trust companies now provide the kind of wealth management services that family offices traditionally have provided for the very wealthy. Many of these smaller trust companies use third-party money managers and deliver returns comparable to other providers, countering the argument that trust company performance is inferior to that of securities firms. The personalized attention and quiet, nonsales tone that mark their service make a compelling case for the trust companies among many affluent clients.

Online Advice

First came discount brokerages. Then came online trading. Now it's online advice. Not only were all three innovations ignored by traditional Wall Street firms when first introduced, they were treated with contempt until their services caught on. "Stocks are sold, not bought," sniffed full-service firms, from 1975, when deregulation made discounting possible, until the mid-1980s, when Schwab and other discounters became permanent and sizable players (and often became the "other" firm with which full-service clients did business).

Online trading was greeted with the same incredulity—why would investors want to tap a keyboard when they could call a broker? Now, about half of all retail stock trading is conducted online, according to the Securities Industry Association. What's next? Advice.

An early entrant, Financial Engines, is a popular Web site among both administrators and participants of 401(k) plans. The Nobel prize–winning mind of William Sharpe backs the investment education provided by Financial Engines, which offers a convenient and thorough experience for employees to manage the choices in their company's retirement plan. Netscape and Silicon Graphics pioneer Jim Clark is behind MyCFO, a more sophisticated online advisor targeting business owners. And former Wheat First Union strategist David Loeper is the chairman of Financeware.com, a service for both investors and advisors that can provide analysis of an existing financial plan—sort of an online second opinion that clients can use to test the values of their plan objectives.

YOUR CURRENT CLIENTS ARE UP FOR GRABS

If greater competition isn't enough to cause anxiety and make you consider focusing on wealth management, consider this: A substantial percentage of affluent clients don't think much of the service they receive from their current financial professional. It's not that they dislike you or hate how you deal with them. The sad fact is that they are neither unhappy nor delighted. This is alarming because it indicates that many clients who appear content may in fact be looking for alternative advisory service—or would accept it if offered.

The central reason why clients don't think much of the service provided by financial professionals is that the service is spotty. Advisors invariably spend a lot of time wooing a prospect and serving them once they become a client, and then gradually start to ignore them.

How often do advisors talk to clients? We wanted to find out, so we did some research with Prince & Associates, which canvassed a cross section of financial advisors—full-service stockbrokers, insurance agents, banks, and independent advisors. To minimize variations by type of service, researchers used a single event around which to gauge advisor attention to clients. They picked the crash of October 1997, when the Dow Industrials lost 554 points. The market break was both dramatic and ironic, coming as it did ten years to the month after the crash of 1987. During the three-day 1997 sell-off, some pundits were saying "the party is over," while others proclaimed that, like the market break a decade earlier, stocks would come roaring back. What were advisors saying and how many were actually in touch with their clients?

The results were startling. Only 18.3 percent—less than one in five—of the advisors surveyed had contacted their clients during the most difficult stock market period in ten years. What could be their excuse? Actually, they had several. (See Figure 2.1.)

Putting out fires. The most common reason provided by advisors—in 75.6 percent of the cases—for not contacting their clients was that they were "busy putting out fires." Lacking a precise definition of what that means (we can safely assume angry clients weren't resorting to arson), we're left with a vision of advisors running around in a panic, dealing with whatever paperwork the market decline caused. That activity prevented them from calling clients.

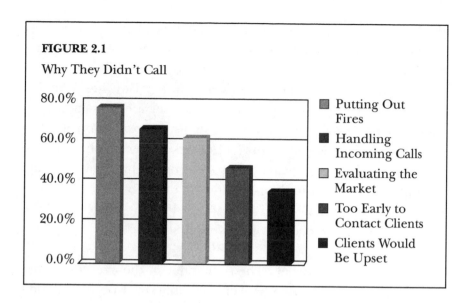

FIGURE 2.1

Why They Didn't Call

Legend:
- Putting Out Fires
- Handling Incoming Calls
- Evaluating the Market
- Too Early to Contact Clients
- Clients Would Be Upset

Assuming clients had initiated the activity, the excuse has some validity, but not much, considering the next most common excuse for not contacting clients.

Handling incoming calls. It seems that 66 percent of advisors claimed to be handling incoming calls. Who did these calls come from? Probably not from affluent clients. Most affluent clients are business owners or professionals who are accustomed to volatility and comfortable with delegating the daily responsibility of account management to their advisors. These clients don't call when the market goes up and down. So who called?

It probably was the advisors' small clients. Encouraged by industry advertising of heady performance returns, small investors seek the opportunities of larger investors. They also want the same level of service. They work to make sure you care about them, so they call. George K., a successful advisor with Merrill Lynch in the Midwest whom we'll meet later, wanted to test the relative service expectations of smaller clients versus his best clients. His assistant logged inbound calls for several months and confirmed the advisor's suspicions: Inbound calls from small clients outnumbered calls from the best clients by a rate of 52 to 3! If, like this advisor, you are busy fielding calls from small clients to such an extent that you cannot reach your best clients, there is a terrible problem with your client service. While the very best clients may not call during a market drop, it is not true that they don't care. They are busy managing their businesses or their careers, the areas they can control. They don't focus on areas such as the stock market over which they have no control. They expect their advisors to be on top of what's happening and to report to them the impact of major changes. If you don't call, you've failed the test of good client service because you've expected the client to make the first move.

Evaluating the market. The remainder of the excuses for not calling clients during the October 1997 market drop reveal additional problems with client service and advisors' perceptions of their roles. The third most common complaint (61.7 percent) among advisors was that they were "busy evaluating the market" and couldn't call their best clients. What precisely were they doing? Rather than defer judgment about this totally unexpected event to professional analysts and portfolio strategists, nearly two-thirds of financial advisors chose to spend time doing their own research, which prevented them from reaching clients.

Too early to contact clients. Ranked fourth (45.6 percent) among the reasons top clients weren't called was that it was "too early to contact clients." Obviously, these advisors were afraid the market would fall further, necessitating more calls and perhaps more rationales for why the market was dropping. As one cynical observer commented, "God forbid the market continued to fall and the advisor might have to make *two* calls!"

Clients would be upset. The last reason advisors didn't call: 35.6 percent said they were afraid "clients would be upset." At first, we attributed the prominence of this reason to the respondents' lack of experience. Rookie advisors, it seems, take greater responsibility for the market's actions and therefore interpret a market downturn as a personal shortcoming—their betrayal of client trust through the offering of bad advice. But that explanation doesn't fit with the actual experience of respondents. Most, it turned out, were established advisors. The real explanation was excuse number three: Advisors were too busy evaluating the market and doing research to call. Apparently, they believed their clients retained them to be the source of market information, and this role extended into an understandable, but errant, assumption of responsibility for the market's decline.

Our findings are troubling for many reasons. Chiefly, they demonstrate advisors' excessive attachment to investments and the stock market. So many of the advisors surveyed defined their role as one of investment advisor and market analyst—to the point of neglecting or ignoring customer service in favor of conducting their own equity research—despite evidence that investing is rarely the chief concern of affluent business owners. Troubling, too, is the fact that while advisors virtually obsess about investing and stock market performance, affluent clients take superior performance for granted (whether or not they should) and believe that investment advisors are commonplace.

WHAT YOUR CLIENTS WANT

Our research shows that affluent business owners want their advisors to help them with the following:

- Retirement planning
- Estate planning, including help with tax issues and trusts
- Investment management, including help with structured products, derivatives, concentrated stock portfolios and options, IPOs, and alternative investments such as hedge funds
- Executive benefits consulting
- Health and/or disability insurance advice and coverage.

WHAT'S THE RIGHT CHOICE FOR YOU?

So after all this, what are you? Are you an investment advisor? A wealth advisor? An investment advisor who wants to become a wealth advisor? Perhaps you're an investment advisor who already is a bit of a wealth advisor? Sometimes the answers don't jump out at us.

Great advisors know the answers to these questions because they truly know their clients and—more important—themselves. How do you perceive and position yourself? Leo J. Pusateri, who heads Pusateri Consulting and Training in Williamsville, New York, says most advisors have not taken enough introspective time to really understand what unique value they bring to client relationships. He believes that advisors should ask themselves a series of simple, but powerful, questions that force them to address what key clients are, or will be, asking. This process leads you down a path of discovery that helps you become more passionate and convincing with clients.

Pusateri's firm, which works with many financial organizations, has created a process called a "value ladder." To use the ladder, the advisor must answer seven questions:

1. Who are you?
2. What do you do?
3. Why do you do what you do?
4. How do you do what you do?
5. Who have you done it for?
6. What makes you different?
7. Why should I do business with you?

"For each of these questions, we have delved into what smart clients are really asking about," Pusateri said. "Ultimately, clients want you to answer these questions with confidence, with passion, and with speed—not glib, canned answers, but nonhesitant answers that demonstrate you've really thought about these things and believe in what you say. Clients and prospects want to feel a specialness and glow about you that comes from truly believing in what you do and loving it. If you hem and haw in your responses or wing them, it's clear you don't know what you're doing or what you want."

Pusateri says it takes four to six months to go through a thorough guided process of self-introspection necessary to get to the answers that work for each advisor. One of the advisors who went through his program said the process brought him to an analysis of his business and himself that he never thought would be possible. Essentially, as Pusateri notes, the end result of the advisor's introspection is a focus on his or her key strengths.

Are your clients attracted to you and staying with you because of your strength as an investment advisor? Or are you breaking out of the investment box and moving toward a broader and more valuable role as a protector and builder of client wealth? Doing that requires a deeper commitment to service, as well as a reevaluation of what service means. Next, we take a closer look at what today's clients want in the way of wealth advisory services.

Investment Advisor or Wealth Advisor Action Checklist

1. If you have decided to remain an investment advisor, are you becoming a true specialist in at least one product or service?

2. If you want to become a wealth advisor, are you taking the appropriate steps:

   - Making regular contact with clients the core of your efforts. This means talking to clients on a scheduled basis regardless of the performance of their investments at the time of the call or visit.

- De-emphasizing short-run market performance in your discussions with clients, as well as downplaying your abilities as a stock picker.
- Learning more about your clients, their families, and the way they look at life so you can recognize their noninvestment financial needs.
- Building your expertise in areas other than investing.

3. Are you making an investment in your own future by taking the time to assess your true strengths and abilities?

Chapter 3

A New Definition of Service

It's all about contact, contact, contact.

Most financial advisors—especially brokers at full-service firms of all sizes—believe they provide superior service. After all, service is what their clients are paying for; with the advent of online brokerage, the price of a trade execution is clearly identifiable at about $20 per trade. Service, therefore, is the key differentiator cited by firms and advisors when asked about the characteristic that distinguishes them from discounters and online brokerages. But what really is the nature of service at a full-service provider? And how good is it?

Service quality for an investment advisor consists of several elements. One, of course, involves the operational and recordkeeping aspects of maintaining a brokerage account. In this sense, service consists of overseeing the accurate and timely delivery of statements and confirmations, and handling sundry administrative chores. Service also consists of access to research and products. But these are ancillary. The core of the full-service brokerage relationship—at least in the view of most affluent investors—is superior performance and personal attention.

Winning Tactic
The Full-Service Formula:

Service = Personal attention and superior performance +
Recordkeeping + Research + Access to products

Since superior performance is exceedingly difficult to deliver on a long-term basis—think of how few money managers consistently beat the S&P 500 Index or other broad-based measure—it would seem that personal attention is the service-differentiating edge most cited by full-service advisors. Ironically, as we have seen, personal attention is often difficult for a full-service advisor to deliver. Trying to attract and serve too many clients often makes it impossible for an advisor to devote sufficient attention to any one client.

Our experience with advisors indicates that clients who express the most satisfaction with their advisor are usually those with whom the advisor keeps in regular contact. How much contact? One respected study says the most highly satisfied clients report they receive an average of 14 contacts with their primary financial advisor over a six-month period. "Contacts" consist primarily of telephone calls, which both advisors and affluent clients agree is the preferred method of keeping in touch, as well as personal meetings, letters, other mailings, and educational programs such as seminars.

Fourteen contacts in six months? Many advisors have reacted with surprise and shock to that number. On the surface, it sounds like a lot. But take a closer look. If an advisor calls a client once a month, meets personally once a quarter, and sends a monthly account review, the total number of semiannual contacts is 14.

Although some clients might prefer fewer contacts or don't have needs that are sufficiently complex to warrant lots of active discussion, advisors still should err on the side of overattentiveness. Dissatisfied clients may not articulate their concerns, and simply will divert assets and cash flow to other advisors. Since clients seem reluctant to house all their assets with one firm anyway, inattentiveness on the part of advisors only serves to reinforce this aversion to asset concentration.

Ironically, the generally low level of advisor service provides an opportunity for those who offer superior service. Investors contacted during market downturns or when their own particular investments perform poorly, invariably reward the attentiveness of their advisors with additional investments. In fact, research shows that almost one-third of clients contacted during the period following the October 1997 market correction turned over additional assets to their primary advisor, which runs counter to the notion that only successful product performance leads to greater asset gathering. On average, these additional investments totaled $260,000—and they came not from cash sitting idly on the sideline but from *another advisor* who was not as diligent in his or her client contact and service. Providing a greater level of service, therefore, pays off in capturing more assets from the same client base. But which services add the most value? That can best be determined by reviewing the service you perform for clients and determining which clients are yielding the greatest return. Here's how one leading advisor conducted such a review and transformed his business.

REVIEW, PARE, AND GROW—A CASE STUDY

In 2001, George K. expects to have $100 million under management from about 50 clients, generating roughly $1 million in gross income. Eventually, he plans to serve 78 clients. This Merrill Lynch financial consultant in the Midwest, who is totally fee based, has adopted Mies van der Rohe's approach to financial consulting: For George, less—in the form of fewer clients and less activity—is more. But it wasn't always this way.

"I've been in the financial services business since 1980. I traded futures in the Chicago pits, but I decided to leave floor trading for the same reasons that drew me there in the first place—the fast pace. When I started I was drawn to the excitement, and originally got a job in Chicago by offering to work for one of the local traders for nothing. But after a while, and seeing people who worked on the floor for 40 years, I decided that trading for a livelihood wasn't for me.

"I had met the president and chief executive of a major industrial company at the club where I played golf, and he asked me to join the company. I worked in various financial positions until 1992. Around 1990, my best friend, who was a Merrill broker in Ohio, started talking to me about how the firm was doing financial planning and consulting. I liked that, because the idea of pounding a stock and calling people out of the blue to sell them something just didn't appeal to me. So when I decided to make a career change as well as a lifestyle change, I took a job with Merrill in another state. My wife and I wanted to move back to the Midwest from Maryland, and we had fallen in love with the town we eventually moved to.

Starting as a Broker

"So there I was in a new city and a new business, not knowing anyone. My wife was very supportive, and understood that I had to spend lots of nights and weekends getting myself established. Since I had had two careers before joining Merrill, I used those as the base of my new business. For the pool of futures traders I had as contacts, I started doing financial plans and conservative stuff. They took enough risk in the way they made their living, so for their retirement accounts and the money they set aside for their children's education, I made very conservative choices. Among the corporate people I formerly worked with—most of whom were in marketing and sales—I did lots of financial plans. That's some of what I had done at the company when I worked there, so these people were very comfortable with me doing that at Merrill Lynch.

"In the early 1990s, financial planning wasn't widely known. I'd do a 60- to 80-page plan for $175, and then come back to discuss how I could fix some of the weaknesses in their current financial position. It was a nice, easy approach.

"In addition to the traders and my former colleagues from industry, I prospected in 'orphan' towns in my state, where there weren't any big-firm brokerages. I would go into a city and invite its leaders—the editor of the local paper, the head of the Chamber of Commerce, a big lawyer—to breakfast. My pitch to them was that I'd commit a day a week to their city and that if I didn't give sufficient value, I would disappear. I wouldn't ask these people to commit to a business relationship, I just wanted to know the names of people I could talk to. I said I would commit 18 months to doing this, and I spent a lot of time meeting CPAs and attorneys over lunch. That approach worked, and I gradually built up a client base.

"By the mid-1990s, I was doing more business and—theoretically—lots of planning. But the reality was that I was out chasing new business rather than implementing what I said I would do in the financial plans we had developed. To help me cover the bases with clients, I borrowed the idea of doing 'batch processing,' which meant that I would talk about trust planning with clients one month followed by another theme the next month. That approach meant I would be able to cover all planning topics with all prospects and clients over a period of a few years. But that didn't work, either, because I was still spending more time selling than advising.

"I finished 1997 with $422,000 in production and $48 million in assets. I had 631 accounts, and I had done 211 Financial Foundations. The reality was that I was using financial planning as a club to get business, and not doing any real planning. I know that the mantra of the brokerage business is that more is better—more accounts, more production, more anything. But I started thinking that maybe more isn't better. I knew I was on a plateau, but doing more seemed to be the wrong approach. I was already doing too much; I was overwhelmed and exhausted, falling into the trap of many others in the business, which is basically promising to do a good job for clients but never getting around to it. I didn't like that.

Serving My Clients

"Like most other brokers when they start, I had good intentions about serving my clients. But the reality was that I wasn't really serving my clients very well. I wasn't able to talk to most of my 631 clients, which I justified by telling myself that if they wanted specific information, they would call. But most of them never did. I knew I had to do something, and I figured out that the most people I could effectively serve would be 100. The big question, of course, was whether 100 people would be enough to make a living from. Then I started doing some homework and began analyzing my business. Believe me, it wasn't easy.

"I started with two reports. The first was production by account. The second was assets per account. I wasn't sure how many households I was serving, but I estimated that it was probably between 200 and 250.

"I tried to figure out my top 100 clients by combining the two lists, but they were dramatically different. From the production list, I found out that I had received fee or commission revenue from 500 accounts in the previous year. This meant that 131 accounts— or more than 16 percent of my book—were effectively inactive. It turned out that more than 90 percent of my production came from just 13 percent of my clients. The funny thing was that I sort of knew this but I had never looked at my business by assets and relationships. I tied names to the accounts and realized that I had a million-dollar account with no production; the guy didn't want to do his securities business with us and just used us for a checking account. I also had a client with small assets but big production."

George and his assistant took the two lists and began to sort the client base, determined to find the best and worst clients. In addition to the 131 clients who were totally inactive in the past year, they found dozens more who had completed one or two transactions, but who had resisted further attempts to learn more about their overall financial picture.

"These people weren't clients, they were buyers. And we were simply salespeople, not advisors. It soon became clear to us that we'd collected a lot of accounts over the years, but relatively few of them had developed into relationships. This was troubling because we want to be advisors to our affluent clients, not just brokers peddling stocks to anyone who calls."

Two Businesses

George began to realize he was operating two different businesses—a brokerage and an advisory service—and that the brokerage business was interfering with his ability to be more effective as an advisor. George's assistant confirmed the time dedication given to the brokerage clients by logging inbound phone calls. She found that calls from small-time brokerage clients outnumbered calls from important advisory clients by a staggering 17:1 ratio. Convinced that culling his clients down to a manageable list of the "best" was the right way to go, George and his assistant developed screens by which they ranked clients.

11 Screens to Finding Your Best Clients

Screening for Your Best Clients

1. Account by production report
2. Value of assets report
3. List of priority clients

4. Likability
5. Approach acceptance
6. Financial wherewithal
7. Premier client capability
8. Hard-dollar profitability
9. Soft-dollar profitability
10. Price-value test
11. Opportunity for future growth

Who were George K.'s best clients? The question was harder to answer than George thought it would be.

"I didn't have any great master plan as to how I would evaluate my client base; it sort of evolved," he said. And what it evolved into was 11 screens.

The screening process, which he began in August 1998, came about in stages. To start, George believed he could find his best 100 clients—his original goal—by using just three screens:

1. A report of each account by production for the first eight months of the year. This was provided by Merrill.
2. The same run by value of assets.
3. A list of priority clients, which by Merrill's definition are accounts where the household has $250,000 in assets at the firm or $5,000 in production for the year. George had 40 such clients.

After he analyzed those three screens, George realized there was little overlap. He began to believe that the "assets at any cost" approach to asset gathering made no sense. One of his accounts, for example, was a small business that kept $3 million in cash in its Working Cash Management Account. "They used us because we were cheaper than a bank, but that's all they did with us. My assistant spent three hours a month with them helping them balance their checkbook."

Realizing he had to go further, George added some subjective screens:

4. Likability. Did he like the client and did the client like him?
5. Which clients believed in George's managed-money approach to investing?
6. Which of the clients had the financial wherewithal to implement the changes recommended in the firm's Financial Foundation plan? He had completed 211 of these at the time.
7. Which clients had *Premier Client* capability, the Merrill term for the client using more of the firm's services?

George believed that if he screened all his clients through these seven filters, the top 100 would jump out. They didn't. Almost all clients were on some of the lists, but no one screen produced the top 100.

"But then I realized I was still thinking in the Merrill, or standard industry, way, which is 'more is better.' I decided to look at my client base as business and think about profitability. So I added three more screens," he said.

8. Hard-dollar profitability. For some clients, George was taking extensive auto and air trips. Travel expenses reduced the profitability of these clients.
9. Soft-dollar profitability. To the hard-dollar costs of serving these clients, George added the cost of his time and that of his assistant.
10. The price-value test. George screened for those clients who demanded a discount in dealing with him.

Finally, he added one more screen:

11. Who provides an opportunity for future growth? Which clients—through referrals, their family business, or the possibility of networking—provided an opportunity for George to increase his business?

"The truth of the matter is that when I was all done after four months, I was still baffled," he said. "We still hadn't reached 100 clients. So I asked my assistant how many clients in the top 150 met all 11 criteria. She went back and figured it out and came up with 33 relationships."

Just 33 Clients

"It took us four months to get to those 11 screens, and when we finally analyzed which clients made it through all 11 filters, we ended up with 33 clients. At first, we thought it was impossible: How could 631 accounts yield just 33 good clients (who represented about 100 accounts)? How could we base a business on 33 clients? So as a joke, we ran a back test. We wanted to see what would have happened to our income in 1998 if we had had just 33 clients. We had to do the number crunching manually, but the results were amazing. The bottom line was that if we had given up all our other clients save those 33, we would have given up just 9 percent of our production! That's right; getting rid of 83 percent of our accounts would have cost us only 9 percent of our gross. Just think of all the time wasted to generate that $39,000 in production. And think of how much more productively that time could have been used had those clients not been clients."

While George realized that it made sense to trim his book down to 33 clients, he still struggled with the "more is better" issue.

"I realized there is a certain comfort in 631 accounts, even though we proved that most of the accounts weren't justifying their existence. Was it better to keep some accounts as 'insurance'?"

George decided it wasn't, and he began to rework his business plan.

"I decided the new plan had to have three elements. First, it needed a single objective. Since being both a broker and an advisor was too unfocused, I decided that my business objective was to create, implement, and monitor life plans. I emphasized life plans because those are more than just a financial plan. A financial plan is too often a product that's done at the beginning of the planning process, put on the shelf, and forgotten. I wanted to separate myself from a product. A life plan is a process.

"Second, my plan had to have a client focus. My 33 clients had passed through all 11 screens, but that 11-part process was too difficult. So I thought a lot about those criteria and boiled them down to three. Now it takes me about 30 minutes to assess whether a client meets these three parameters:

1. I have to like the prospect or prospects and they have to like me.
2. We must legitimately agree on our business and investment philosophy. I use managed accounts, for the most part. If a client doesn't like doing business that way or tries to prove that he's a better money manager than the professional—and I had one client who was constantly sabotaging our relationship that way—then that client is not right for the way I do business. I can't afford to plan for someone who is not going to implement my suggestions.
3. The client must have the wherewithal to implement the recommended courses of action."

Handing Off Clients

But what about the clients who didn't meet George's criteria? He decided that they would have to go.

"Fortunately, Merrill has opened several Investor Service Group (ISG) centers around the country, staffed by salaried registered personnel, who handle smaller clients. I moved several of my accounts to the ISG and sent a letter along with the notice to explain what I was doing. The compliance department cut out a lot of what I wanted to say, including the personal stuff. But I essentially told them that if they hadn't heard from me in a long time they deserved better service than I was able to give them, and that the new arrangement would provide it. Some people called me and complained, and there were some rough conversations, but a lot fewer than I thought there would be. I couldn't convince some people that I was doing the right thing for them—and some said I was a horse's rear—but in my heart I knew I was doing the right thing. And I think they now know that.

"I also wondered how the 33 remaining clients were going to react to my change of business. How was I going to present the new concept to them? My biggest worry was that each of the 33 would wonder where they were in the pecking order and start thinking that they might be the next client to be cut—and if so, would it be better if they got out now.

"I thought the smartest thing to do would be to discuss the change with my best client—the one with whom I have the best relationship, and who enjoys mentoring. This client is in his mid-60s and has owned a manufacturing company for 35 years. I took him to lunch and explained the whole thing for three hours. He sat there quietly. After I finished my explanation, I asked what he thought. He started by telling me a story.

"He said that his business causes him to have a nightmare that once or twice a year wakes him up in a sweat. In his dream, his factory, which makes marine propellers, runs out of raw material and everything stops dead. Because of that nightmare—and because he realizes that if he runs out of raw materials his business would be decimated—he said he keeps a minimum of four suppliers in the game. Two are domestic and two are foreign. He realizes that keeping four suppliers doesn't make sense, but since he can't really rely on any of them, he uses four because it makes him feel comfortable.

"Then he told me that none of his suppliers ever made a commitment to supply him with raw materials the way that I was planning to commit to serving him. He said he would be embarrassed not to give a supplier all his business if that supplier were committed to him in that way. He suggested that I tell all my 33 best clients about what I was planning to do, just as I told him. So I did.

"I met for two- and three-hour conversations and explained my plan to all of them. I told everyone I was making a huge commitment to this new way of doing business and asked them to help me fill those 45 other slots, which would bring my total client list to 78. If they didn't help me, I explained, I'd be right back where I was before, which was scrambling to get clients and not being able to give them attention. In many ways, my new approach to business was a lot like changing one's eating habits rather than going on a diet: I wasn't just cutting out fat, I was changing everything I did.

"I told my 33 clients that I would welcome their referrals and spend 30 minutes with anyone they sent me. But I also told them that if the referral didn't fit my new regimen and made me cheat on the way I do business, I wouldn't take on their referral as a client. I'd take him to another financial professional who can best serve him, but I wanted to make sure that my clients wouldn't be hurt if I did that. Happily, they went along with me."

The New Practice

Here's how George K. serves his clients now. Based on Merrill survey data that encompass the experiences and preferences of top clients, the firm found that clients feel most satisfied when advisors use a 12/4/2 client contact system. The numbers signify the following: All priority clients receive 12 personal contacts a year. In addition to those monthly contacts, the client receives four portfolio reviews annually, of which two are completed in person. George took that formula and modified it. He kept the 12 personal contacts, but makes four in-person visits instead of two, and two portfolio reviews instead of four. In fact, he believes personal contact is so valuable that he added one more personal contact—a full-day meeting—to the annual agenda for his best clients.

"I told these top clients that I wanted to be sure that I was serving their interests completely, and that I wanted to learn more about their businesses and personal lives. Most of them were taken aback initially, either because they thought I wasn't serious or because

they thought I had a boondoggle in mind, like an all-day golf out-
ing. But I had a serious, breakfast-through-dinner session in mind.
I wanted to spend a day at their workplace, at home, and over
meals getting to know what's important in their lives and perhaps
helping them in ways they never considered before."

The clients humored George and let him hang around their offices and company headquarters. Sometimes he sat in on meetings,
other times he wandered the business premises and talked to key
people, such as controllers and legal counsel. He met friends and
business associates. While both family and business colleagues expressed surprise initially at George's presence, they quickly
warmed to the idea. They often asked him questions about the
market and investing. In addition to learning more about the
clients and the potential for additional services, George immediately differentiated his level of service from that of any competitor.

"No one else was offering to spend a whole day with clients," he
said. This didn't go unnoticed by clients' friends and colleagues.
Within the first few months of his full-day meetings, George had
three multi-million-dollar clients by referral. He is convinced his
physical presence made these referrals possible. Today, all
prospecting is done as a by-product of his one-day meetings.

"Sometime during the meeting, I ask my clients just two or three
questions. First, I ask if they are happy with my service. If they say
they are, I ask whether they think it would behoove me to prospect
more people in their industry. Usually they say it would. Then I ask
the following question and shut up: 'If you were in my shoes, and
knowing what you know about me and my business, how would you
go about prospecting in your industry?' I let them think about it
and come up with a response."

George's best client—the marine propeller manufacturer—invited him to come along to a major trade show in Chicago. Walking the vast McCormick Place exhibit hall with George at his side,
the client introduced the advisor to several friends in the business,
explaining that George was his financial advisor. George followed
up later and several of those he visited became clients.

Regular Appointments

George, who calls himself a comprehensive financial planner, says the culling process has enabled him to create a client management system that lets him devote the appropriate time to everyone he serves. He knows who he must phone each month, as well as who he will visit. He also knows that over two years' meetings, he will cover all the necessary planning topics he needs to review with his clients. He establishes a standing monthly appointment for each client, giving them a morning or an afternoon slot "for the rest of their lives." He says that fewer than 20 percent of the appointments take place at the allotted time, but they are scheduled nonetheless, just like regular dental appointments. George also leaves two full days a month wide open for rescheduling purposes. His assistant calls to confirm three business days before each phone appointment and eight days before an in-person meeting.

"The process is mine. It enables me to focus on the monthly theme area, and it allows my clients and me to sleep well every night. We rarely talk about the stock market or any particular investment. My clients are not all that interested in investments as such; they are interested in investments as tools to get them where they want to be. The reality is that taxes, estate planning, life insurance, whether they are a C corporation or an S corporation, and other factors are more important than a particular stock or bond."

But what about clients who still want to trade and who like the excitement of the stock market? George doesn't have many such clients, but he will be the first to admit that while some clients buy into the managed money approach, they find it boring.

"For them, we create a slush fund, and I use that and other gambling terms on purpose. The slush fund is a separate subaccount that I'm not accountable for and on which I don't have opinions. They can use Merrill Lynch Online directly or go through my office and deal solely with one of my assistants. I give them Merrill Lynch research if they want it, but since I can add no value in this area of the business, I don't offer any advice or opinions. In total, only about eight or nine of my clients have slush funds, and the spring 2000 decline in high-tech stocks washed out a lot of the high fliers."

With average client assets at $1.6 million and a return on assets of about 1 percent, George sees himself leaving transaction-oriented, less wealthy clients to other advisors. He also sees the team approach as an avenue he would be unlikely to explore, at least at present.

"I'm a real control freak, so I don't think a team makes sense for me. I've developed my own business model, and I want to stick with it. There certainly are other paths to take, but I think for advisors to be successful going forward, they must pick their own business objective and live it passionately; they have to believe and act on the belief that more is not better, and they have to change their outlook. What I've done is a lifestyle change, it's not a diet."

Winning Tactic

If you were able to devote a block of several hours, or even an entire workday, to one client, how do you think your relationship with that client would be affected? Getting to know a client in such depth, do you think he or she would feel more comfortable entrusting more assets to you? Referring wealthy friends to you? Having you solve more problems for him and his family?

OTHER CONTACT IDEAS

Since George's approach may not necessarily work for you, consider customer contact ideas from other advisors. All of these suggestions are likely to work in your attempt to increase contact with your clients and improve service. In many cases, however, advisors are coming to understand that no matter how hard they work, they alone cannot provide the service their clients demand. Advisors are discovering that serving the affluent successfully requires assistance. In our next chapter, we'll discuss how to get the assistance you need whether you decide to remain a solo practitioner or whether you decide you might be more productive working as part of a team.

On-site meetings. Steve H., a wirehouse advisor in Boston, makes a point of meeting with clients on their turf for their quarterly and annual updates. "Clients don't expect you to travel to see them, but you should," he says. "It's their money, and they're paying you to manage it. What's the problem with going to their office or their home? Ninety-nine percent of my client meetings are conducted outside my office, even if I have to travel a ways to do it."

Birthday meetings. Chuck R., a wirehouse advisor in North Carolina, holds client meetings immediately after the client's birthday. He does this for two reasons. He says it prompts clients to be more open and forthcoming with him because they sense the passage of time when they meet soon after a personal milestone. Second, it keeps them from fixating on performance, which would be the natural subject if they meet to discuss the results of the previous quarter. "The focus is on you," he tells his clients, "not on the calendar."

Regular e-mails. Steve B., an independent advisor in Colorado, keeps in regular touch with clients through e-mail. Every Monday, he e-mails a 500-word market commentary to all his clients who use e-mail. "It keeps communications lines open and gives the client an opportunity to reply. And it saves me a tremendous amount of time," he says. Clients can respond at their own pace, and Steve says he receives fewer phone calls as a result. A new client said that he had never heard from a broker as frequently as he did until he hired Steve.

Media contact. This is an unusual, but effective, form of "contact." Bill C., an advisor with a regional firm near Columbus, Ohio, is the financial editor of a monthly magazine in his suburb. Because Bill is already active in the community, the regular magazine appearances do as much to cement his ties to existing clients as they do to attract new clients. The 12 yearly contacts his client-readers receive are made more powerful because the message appears in an independent publication, not something Bill produced himself.

Newsletters. Dave J. is an independent advisor in California. His specialty is retirement planning, and he targets prospects who are three to five years away from retirement. He captures prospects through seminars and referrals and doesn't let them slip through his fingers during the time until retirement. Dave keeps the prospect active in his contact management system and puts him on a subscriber list to receive regular newsletters about retirement. "I may not speak to the prospect for three years, but the newsletters usually make them think of me—and not turning to the yellow pages—when they decide they need a financial advisor," he said.

The 11-Step Process Action Checklist

Would you like to see what would happen to your business if you were to put through George K.'s 11-step, client analysis process? How much revenue would you lose if you were to concentrate your efforts on a limited number of key clients? Answer these questions to get an idea of which clients—and how many of them—you might shed in order to devote more time to your remaining clients.

1. Rank client accounts by revenue.

2. Rank client accounts by assets.

3. List "priority" accounts—those designated as premier accounts by your firm based on revenue, assets, or other criteria.

4. Rank clients by likability. Include comments from your sales assistant and others in your office, if appropriate.

5. List clients by how closely they are in sync with your investment style. If you are an advocate of separately managed accounts, for example, how many of your clients believe strongly in this approach? If you love the options market, to take another example, how many of your clients share your interest?

6. List your clients by wealth. This may involve taking some calculated guesses. But if you surmise that several of your clients are just giving you a small portion of their assets, there may be lots more to tap if you were to concentrate your efforts.

7. List clients who buy more than one service from you. As we discovered, clients who have a multifaceted relationship with you tend to be the most loyal clients.

8. List clients who are expensive to maintain in terms of hard dollars. Visiting some clients may require travel, for instance, while others may demand costly gifts.

9. Do the same analysis for the soft costs of serving your clients. Some clients may require excessive administrative support, which can be costly in terms of time, as well as being a drain on the spirit.

10. List which clients demand discounts.

11. List which clients have the best networks of their own. These are clients who, if satisfied, can mention you to other wealthy individuals.

Chapter 4

*W*hen One Isn't Enough

> *To do everything clients require, do you become a team builder or a team member? And where do you turn when you need more?*

We've reviewed the kind of service today's wealthy clients demand, as well as the motivation of these clients for seeking financial solutions. Still, two pieces of the successful financial advisor puzzle are missing: (1) What, specifically, do these clients need in terms of products, services, and information, and (2) how can a lone advisor meet those needs?

We mentioned some of the financial needs of today's affluent clients in Chapter 2. But to give you a comprehensive overview of these needs, let's look at the big picture. (See Figure 4.1.)

QUESTIONS TO ASK CLIENTS

The big picture is a framework for probing clients about the current state of their financial health and their need for financial prod-

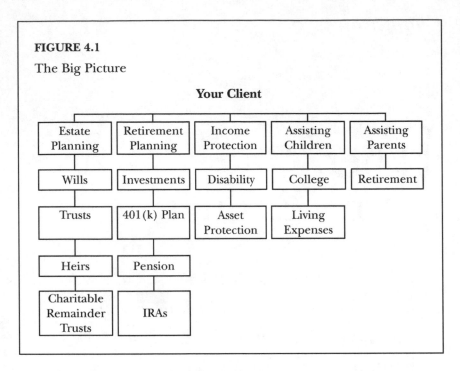

FIGURE 4.1

The Big Picture

ucts and services. It is also a diagnostic tool that reveals your ability to deliver those products and services. Let's look at the questions you should be asking your clients regarding each of their major financial needs.

Questions to Ask Regarding Estate Planning

- Do you have a current will?
- Do you have a living will?
- Do you have a durable power of attorney in the event you can't make decisions?
- Who are the beneficiaries of your estate?
- Do you have guardians for your children?
- Do you have trustees for your estate?
- Do you own life insurance? How much? What kind? Who are the beneficiaries?
- Do you have a succession plan for your business?

Questions to Ask Regarding Retirement Planning

- When did you last do an asset allocation plan?
- What do you hope to do in retirement?
- Where do you plan to live?
- How much do you have in your retirement plan?
- How are these assets invested?
- How much do you think you'll need?
- Are you on track to reach your goals?
- Do you have long-term care insurance?
- Do you have any annuities?
- Do you know how you will draw down your retirement funds?
- Do you know the details of your employer's plan?
- Do you know how much you'll be receiving from Social Security and Medicare?

Questions to Ask Regarding Income Protection

- Do you have disability insurance? How much?
- When do your disability benefits begin?
- What is the maximum monthly disability income you could receive and for how long would you receive it?
- Do you have additional disability coverage?
- Have you ever been sued?
- Does your business have adequate protection against lawsuits for sexual harassment, product liability, and worker's compensation claims?

Questions to Ask Regarding Assisting Children

- Have you saved for your children's college education? How much?
- Do your children have their own savings accounts? Do they have Roth IRAs? UGMA accounts?

- Do you provide financial assistance for grown children? Do you expect that support to continue?
- Do you have any grandchildren? Do you assist them today? Do you plan to provide for them in the future?
- Are there special needs? Child support? Providing for step-children? Provisions for foster children, nieces, nephews, children with disabilities?

Questions to Ask Regarding Assisting Parents

- What are the ages of your parents? Your grandparents?
- How is their health?
- How will your parents provide for their expenses in retirement? Do they have long-term health care insurance?
- Do you provide care for any older relatives or friends? Are there any for whom you might one day be responsible?

ANALYZING YOUR ROLE

The totality of need among affluent clients is great. Can you adequately and comfortably provide advice in all these areas? If you're typical of advisors who come from the securities industry, you probably feel confident helping clients plan for retirement, especially selecting investments used to fund IRAs and other accounts. If your formative business years were spent in insurance or financial planning, your comfort zone typically involves income protection and elder care issues. And if you have legal training or trust company experience, estate planning is likely the area where you feel the most confident. But outside your area of experience, you may feel uncomfortable purporting to be an expert or recommending financial solutions. How do you bridge the gap and provide expertise you don't possess yourself? There are several possibilities.

If you are a generalist and wish to work alone, you can use the resources of your firm and third parties to provide expertise in specialized areas. Most wirehouses offer in-firm experts in estate planning, insurance, restricted stock sales, and other specialized areas. Some wirehouse consultants, such as George K., who we met earlier, rely on outside investment managers, and position themselves to clients as a "manager of managers." Other consultants remain independent but develop a referral network that may include a local estate attorney and an accountant.

In this chapter, we're going to discuss different ways to expand your business beyond the grasp of your own ten fingers. We'll first discuss teams, and then ways to reach out and develop the resources you need outside your own firm or team.

WHY TEAMS MAKE SENSE

Many consultants—and their firms—now realize that no single person can provide all the expertise a wealthy individual requires. For that reason, firms are supporting consultants' efforts to create teams. Stanley O'Neal, President of Merrill Lynch's U.S. Private Client Group, told the Securities Industry Association's annual convention that consultant teams are now an integral part of the way the giant firm plans to serve wealthy clients. In his remarks, in fact, O'Neal noted that Merrill is no longer in the retail securities business; it's in the wealth management business.

If you are a generalist and wish to create your own team, the logical choice of teammate(s) would be one or more specialists. These could be product specialists—a municipal bond expert, perhaps, or an insurance and annuity specialist, or maybe an options trader. Or they could be service specialists, perhaps handling restricted stock transactions or selling 401(k) plans to small businesses. Often, these specialists have developed a considerable following among clients who need their expertise—and who also may need yours.

We've identified four team models that have achieved success with affluent clients.

The financial coach. One of the greatest positioning statements in financial services belongs to Meespierson, an investment management boutique in the Netherlands. This rapidly growing firm says it "helps entrepreneurs become investors." The model is a team that focuses on the development of the client. In Canada, Richard Claydon and Jock Macdonald of Loring Ward stress education, with a new topic for clients to consider at every meeting. Finally, independent advisor and *On Wall Street* magazine columnist Lewis Walker helps clients understand the complexities and risks of wealth and estate needs prior to accepting any assignment.

The champions. Giants like Merrill Lynch and Salomon Smith Barney have extensive capabilities to serve the wealth management needs of affluent clients. But their vast array of services is daunting, even to their savviest advisors. As an entity, a firm can meet every need, but someone must direct the players. Too often, brokers are unwilling to access a firm's internal resources for fear of losing credibility or control.

Enter the Champion. He or she is a strong personality who literally "commands" the army of internal specialists to craft client solutions. Seated on the same side of the table as the client, the Champion asks questions and drives hard bargains for the client. Everyone at headquarters and in the service areas of a firm knows that the Champion gets his or her way—and that the firm and clients ultimately benefit.

My team. A true team expands your advisory horizons—allowing your practice to be more things to more people. A successful team combines the skills of an investment professional with those of a financial planner or estate-planning specialist. Bigger teams add experts in alternative investments or retirement plans. Clients typically enter such a practice to solve one problem and are introduced to other team members when other needs arise. Some teams are "virtual" in that team members are not with the same firm but work in close affiliation.

The company. Reminiscent of the old IBM and Xerox selling teams, the company model is growing rapidly at the upper end of the wealth management market. Goldman Sachs and J.P. Morgan successfully unite client service specialists, investment bankers, capital markets professionals, and, in the case of Morgan, succession and estate planners. These teams travel together and typically meet repeatedly with clients to assure full and immediate attention to a single integrated strategy. The ultra-high-net-worth (UHNW) market demands this level of complex service, and companies are scrambling to train teams to improve tactics. Top UHNW teams carry an air of confidence about them.

Winning Tactic

As the complexity of clients' financial needs grows, you improve your chances of success when you prove that your personal organization can fully address client needs.

A TALE OF TWO TEAMS

Two of the nation's most prestigious financial firms—one with roots in investment banking and the other in commercial banking—are leaders in the team approach. Let's look at how they view the team process.

The Investment Bank Approach

Joe K. has been with one of America's most prestigious investing banking firms for two years. Earlier, the 44-year-old held marketing and strategic planning posts at a Fortune 500 company. The group he is now part of was created in 1998 to serve very high-net-worth clients.

"We work at the very upper echelon of wealth. Our clients are centimillionaires at a minimum; most have assets north of $200 million," Joe says, explaining that the firm handles services traditionally provided by private banks, and adds the services of a full-service investment bank. "Private banks seldom conduct direct brokerage, but we do. We operate more like an institutional service business than an individual business—actually, more like the tax-aware institutional model."

Joe's business unit provides full asset allocation services and estate planning. It also engages in restricted stock sales, hedging, collars, and other equity techniques—but not real estate or trust-like personal services such as writing checks and disbursing payments. Some clients maintain relationships with the firm as well as with a trust bank. Joe and his colleagues work in two- to four-person teams responsible for identifying wealthy prospects and bringing them to the firm. The teams also bring together the resources of the firm to assess the client's needs and tailor a program.

"Our name opens the door, since it has much more prestige than a large brokerage firm. Most of our leads come from our investment banking activities; we don't cold-call millionaires. We try to leverage the relationships of investment banks and try to get their clients to at least listen to us—it doesn't cost them anything to do that. We explain what we do, and many prospects decide to use us because our business model is compelling. We simply charge a competitive management fee on the portfolio. There is no charge for our advice."

Once a prospect becomes a client—usually the top executive of a company that has gone through an IPO—the firm puts the proceeds in a money market account.

"Most new centimillionaires like to count their money in the first 30 days," Joe notes. "We can then take many months to invest the cash."

Joe says that his lack of previous financial industry experience has not been a hindrance.

"As long as you demonstrate that you are trustworthy and credible, the clients are satisfied. The fact that I had been a seasoned executive elsewhere and that I am not a rogue individual making decisions from the hip obviously helps. We have a disciplined process at our firm that brings all its resources to bear."

He says some of his 20 to 25 clients—the maximum permissible under the team approach—are demanding, while some "can't be bothered knowing the details of their financial lives. Many lead active lives, and sometimes we have to work to track them down."

The team provides quarterly in-person reviews, and does not offer the ability for clients to check their accounts or portfolios online. Some clients handle a portion of their investments online, but very few.

"At the end of the day, we bring several things to the table. We bring the reputation of our firm, which is unique in the industry. We focus exclusively on wealth management, and we're paid only on assets under management. We're high service and high touch. The vast majority of our clients were CEOs at one point in their lives and are used to making decisions. All they have to do is choose us."

The Trust Company Approach

Trisha Stewart is co-head of J.P. Morgan's Advice Lab for private clients. The group supports client-servicing teams by providing the analysis required to meet the complex client needs of each team's roughly 200 clients.

"The Morgan approach is to deliver an integrated service to high-net-worth individuals. We organize a team around the client. The five- or six-person teams usually are directed by private bankers who are the lead relationship managers. Also on the team are brokers, investment managers, portfolio managers, trust and estate specialists, and service specialists," said the Morgan vice president, who noted that the client's primary contact actually may be one of the team specialists, rather than the generalist. Teams cut across the bank's legal structure, including members who technically are employees of the trust company, the commercial bank, or the broker-dealer unit.

The service is designed to give the client the best product-neutral advice. The bank doesn't charge a single fee, but rather several fees depending on the services used. She noted that a client with $100 million at the bank who does not need or want Morgan to do very much would pay much less than a client with $15 million who asks the team to do a lot.

"Since many of our clients have significant wealth concentrated in one stock, we often look at asset allocation and see whether the client's assets are structured in the best way possible. On occasion, we will charge for a full-fledged financial plan, but by and large we don't charge for that," Stewart said.

In addition to applying analytic tools to determine risk in client portfolios and developing new ways to analyze their stock options, Stewart's unit also will assess situations unique to a particular client, such as the tax advantages of holding an asset in one of several ways. Stewart says clients come to Morgan through its investment banking activities, as well as through referrals from clients and from the legal and accounting professionals the firm uses.

In this field, Morgan competes against investment banking firms and the high-end private banking community. Local banks may provide Morgan's clients with the payroll, cash management, and other day-to-day services their businesses require, but local banks "tend not to have the ability to lend against $50 million in stock," Stewart says.

To get closer to its clients, Morgan operates regional offices, where it takes on the local color. Team members in Texas and Silicon Valley, for example, rarely wear suits like their New York counterparts. In fact, one team member in California warned a visiting investment banker not to come in "Wall Street attire" lest he tip off Silicon Valley about an impending deal. In all, about 200 bank professionals work on the client teams.

"One important differentiating factor is the high degree of pro-active communication that JPM shares with its clients, whether it be a discussion of changing market conditions, of goals and objectives, or just touching base. The relationship with Morgan is highly personal," she says.

At a minimum, clients receive quarterly contact in the method they prefer—in person, over the phone, or by mail. An in-depth session is held once a year.

"We have clients who don't call for six months, then call every day. Clients who use us primarily for brokerage can call us four times a day. Clients for whom we manage money meet with us once a year. Some want us to maintain a brick wall between their personal and business affairs, while there are others for whom the personal and business are intertwined. We can do whatever they want."

When money management is involved, Morgan does most of it in-house.

"For product we don't offer, we'll go outside to get the best available. One group of funds we use is American Century, of which Morgan owns 45 percent. We'll also try to diversify the client's holdings. Even though we know that most of our clients don't have 100 percent of their wealth with us (or with any one provider), at least we know that we won't be duplicating their holdings," Stewart said. "The client teams are anchored by people who have been in business for a long time. We want to build relationships, listen, and solve problems. Most of us love to roll up our sleeves and make things better for clients."

THE CLIENT-CREATED TEAM

Sometimes, learning how to work in a team is necessary even if you haven't yet formed your own team. Truly affluent clients often develop their own team, a "virtual" family office, in effect, consisting of a few close advisors. These, typically, include a CPA, estate attorney, business insurance agent, and banker. If your background is in investments, you can work successfully as part of the client's team only when you understand each team member's power over the business owner.

Mort A., an advisor with a regional securities firm in Buffalo, New York, learned the importance of advisor dynamics the hard way. He received a referral from an attorney he had befriended, who had been retained by a couple who had just won big in the New York State Lottery. The new millionaires came from very humble backgrounds and were intimidated by their new wealth and the complexity of managing it. They had turned to the attorney for help, and the attorney had turned to Mort.

Mort was invited to a meeting by the attorney, where they, the couple, and an accountant, would discuss the couple's plans. Mort was given the opportunity to present his thoughts for the couple, who seemed very pleased with his recommendations for investing the money. When the accountant rejected the advice as "risky," Mort was stunned, the couple was chagrined, and the attorney was noncommittal.

"I violated one of the key rules of working as a team with other advisors," Mort admitted after the meeting. "Before presenting the idea to the couple, I should have run the idea past the attorney and the accountant to make sure they understood what I was recommending and why."

Mort had a hunch that the accountant did not fully comprehend the investment concept, which involved tax deferral and an investment program. So he suggested to the accountant that they meet privately before meeting again with the couple, and the accountant agreed. In that separate meeting, Mort was able to explain his concept to the accountant who acknowledged that he hadn't understood the investment program Mort was recommending and admitted that most of his clients did not have the wealth that made such a program sensible. At the next client meeting, Mort proposed the idea again, the accountant approved it, and Mort won the account.

Teams and You Checklist

If you are like most advisors, you work neither for one of the nation's premier investment banks nor for one of its leading commercial bank competitors. You may be at a firm where teams are increasingly encouraged, or at least not discouraged. If so, consider the following steps:

1. If you have a product specialty, consider forming an alliance with one or two other product specialists and a generalist to round out your team.

2. Similarly, if you are a generalist, bolster your offerings with teammates who are specialists.

3. If you are strong in generating new business, team up with an advisor whose personality and experience lean toward internal customer service. You will help your new teammate attract new business he or she might never bring in, while you are likely to retain more clients than you had in the past.

4. Consider a cross-generational team. If you are starting out, you can help a more senior advisor by assuming some of the administrative or customer-care responsibilities. If you are a more senior advisor, consider adding a younger advisor just starting out who might take care of the customer-service aspects of the business while you seek new clients or greater assets from existing clients.

5. Look outside your firm for noncompeting teammates with complementary skills. For example, while many

accountants are entering the wealth advisory business—as we'll see in our next chapter—there are still
tax specialists and other accounting professionals who
will welcome your referrals and refer clients to you in
return. Attorneys who specialize in estate planning are
other potential informal teammates.

GOING BEYOND TEAMS

Sometimes, even a well-designed team can't cover enough ground
to provide clients with all they need. Advisors are learning they
must go outside of their own teams and their own firm to provide
the services and information their clients require. Going "outside,"
however, raises the issue of trust. Since top advisors and their clients are the envy of the financial services world, advisors cannot
casually trust others with access to their valued clients unless some
formal or informal reciprocal relationship exists among all parties.
For example, an advisor may not entrust his clients to a CPA unless
the accountant also entrusts his clients to the advisor for investment and wealth management advice in return. The same guide-
line holds true for attorneys, many of whom have provided estate
planning and investment services for your clients. In the future,
strategic alliances among financial professionals will be more defined, more objective, and more likely to be subject to written con-
tracts or letters of understanding among the involved parties. But
no contract can by itself create the most important feature of a true
alliance, which is joint economic need.

There are three primary models for financial advisors and potential strategic partners. All three are based on the economic value
each party brings to the alliance and depend on ongoing contributions to ensure long-term success.

The Referral Model

Here, each party to the alliance provides new business referrals to the other alliance partner. Unlike loose-knit, "I-give-you-one-you-give-me-one" arrangements of the past, the referral model is structured as a professional marketing alliance. Written objectives, time lines, and benchmarks for review are the key features of a good alliance. In addition, the agreement contains a provision for dissolving the alliance and assigning clients to each partner.

Many advisors have resisted such formal trappings, claiming they don't want to be locked in to restrictive deals with other professionals, or that such a level of formality is unnecessary. In truth, many relationships really may not require such formal measures. As in a prenuptial agreement, the party with the most to lose is the party with the most at risk—and the most in need of protection. Given the difficulty and expense of finding affluent clients, most advisors would be well served to have protection.

Agreements also should bind the firm with which the CPA or attorney in question is associated, not just the individual professional. Countless clients have been lost to firms after the retirement or death of the advisor's key contact. No longer protected by the departed partner, an alliance may be all too quickly dismantled by surviving partners who have their own relationships.

In addition to specific written agreements, there are other ways to control referral partners. One outstanding example was developed by Mort A., our advisor in Upstate New York. Each January, Mort sends a personalized letter to each client in which he states his group's commitment to the client and to the arduous task of tax preparation to be completed in the months ahead. The letter asks for written permission to share account information with each client's tax and estate professionals in order to streamline the process and allow the client to remain peripheral to the detail work. With copies of the signed letter sent on to each of his client's CPAs and estate attorneys, Mort has reinforced his leadership of the clients' advisors—both to the clients and to the other professionals.

Most large brokerage firms and insurance providers have some form of referral program in place for CPAs. But the assumption too often made by the creators of these formal plans is that the CPA firms will remain constant in their development as advisory firms; that the CPAs will become accustomed to providing referrals and receiving income without doing much work. The securities firms sponsoring these arrangements have underestimated the potential for CPA firms to offer their own expanded range of services in addition to traditional accounting. Client control and higher profit margins are powerful incentives to the CPA firms to expand directly into the securities business—and simply withdraw from current alliances with brokers.

The Extended Service Offerings Model

Alliances created to provide specific services among two or more professionals are known as *extended service offerings*. Some of the most productive relationships in financial services are based on this model. In insurance, an example of this model is the way a specialist in the sale of long-term care policies skillfully joins forces with a provider of investment management accounts to help affluent clients provide for retirement savings and risk protection. The client benefits from a comprehensive solution to a problem from two experts. Another example is Steve H., our wirehouse advisor in Boston, who maintains strong ties to a local estate-planning firm to whom he regularly introduces new clients. In turn, the estate firm refers its clients to Steve when they have a need in his specialty— investment management consulting.

Extended service offerings should be governed by explicit agreements. Done correctly, an extended service offering creates an impressive and powerful alliance. But without a solid understanding of each party's responsibilities, arrangements with other service providers can be more tenuous than straight referral arrangements. Partners in extended service ventures can become proprietary about the clients each delivers; disputes often arise over the "ownership" of clients referred under the arrangement.

Key issues involved in structuring agreements in an extended service offering include:

- *Operational issues.* The actual services and products offered by each party, fees, location of client assets, methods of transfer, and the nature and content of reporting to the client.
- *Service issues.* Type of presentations and meetings, and frequency of client meetings and attendees.
- *Marketing issues.* How will prospects be introduced, what are the expectations for prospects, ratio of conversion to clients, closed clients, and revenues per client.
- *Noncompete and dissolution provisions.* These should be clear to avoid the tendency for alliance partners to cherry-pick the best clients from among the referrals.

The Vendor Management Model

Perhaps the best alliance partner for a successful advisor is a vendor. After all, their success—because their products are sold through intermediaries like you—depends on your success. They are extremely unlikely to change marketing channels (such as switching a fund from the broker-sold channel to the no-load direct channel). Increased competition among mutual fund companies, separate account managers, and variable annuity firms has been a boon for top advisors seeking support for their practices.

Vendors prefer productive relationships. Most of all they prefer a relationship with a top advisor who accounts for a significant aggregation of assets, rather than a passel of relationships to acquire the same volume of assets. Just as an advisor wants fewer, wealthier clients, vendors want fewer, more productive advisors.

In return for these relationships, vendors often can provide business-building expertise through product or practice-management training. Many fund and investment management firms will offer a top advisor the services of a portfolio manager for client presentations and review meetings, which can be a huge boost to your prestige in the eyes of clients. In addition, vendors are a good source of funding for your direct-marketing efforts. Often, they will provide cash for seminars, mailings, and client meetings. Anxious to woo top advisors, they also have provided training in advanced marketing techniques, invitations to exclusive marketing conferences, and the direct subsidy of professional sales coaching programs.

In addition to the product training they provide to all reps, vendors also conduct "value-added" programs that go beyond the basics for top advisors. These educational offerings teach advisors about new products and new markets, imparting business-building skills such as "sales tactics for the affluent" and "practice valuation." Often developed with the aid of industry experts, value-added programs help companies improve their relationships with advisors by deepening their commitment beyond product. The best advisors take advantage of this support and adapt each program to the needs of their practices.

Several vendors now offer very compelling value-added programs to aid advisors. By doing so, they have increased their stature among leading advisors and their firms. One of the earliest entries was the Innovative Heritage Planning series introduced by MFS. Heritage helped advisors focus on the financial planning needs of their clients, and took a leadership role while brokerage firms wrestled with how to best provide such consultative tools. Later value-added programs rode the tail of the bull market in the latter years of the 1990s. Putnam and Lord Abbett trumpeted the bull market boom through high-profile pundits Dr. Bob Goodman and Jack McCarthy.

AIM Funds, which has created a series of comprehensive business development programs under the "Essentials" umbrella, upped the vendor ante by associating with best-selling author Harry Dent. The author's "Roaring 2000s" forecasts and books spotlight the powerful demographic forces propelling the market. AIM developed funds based on Dent's views, and he works with AIM and its wholesalers in their efforts to support the retail distribution system.

As the bull market matured, other fund companies sought programs to provide noninvestment practice management support. In late 1998, Van Kampen Funds introduced a training program in high-net-worth client sales known as "Nine Lives of the Affluent," based on compelling research of wealthy clients by Russ Alan Prince of Prince & Associates, who also developed the innovative "Advisor 2000" for Prudential Investments. Alliance Capital rolled out a value-added entry featuring valuation expert Mark Tibergien of Moss Adams, who sought to educate independent investment advisors about the value of their practices. One of the most successful initiatives was developed by John Bowen when he was at Assante RWB Advisory Services. He provided a "Fast Start" series for advisors seeking to transition from sales commissions to a fee-based practice. Bowen then added the "Personal CFO" training for more advanced players.

Other companies sought holes in the training offered by their target distributors. Conseco Fund Group's Bruce Johnston provided Merrill Lynch financial consultants with specialized programs in presentation skills, the Internet, and in client prospecting techniques— all adaptable to the needs of a branch or sales district. The quality of these value-added programs has increased dramatically, propelled by both the investments of several forward-looking product companies and by the insights of savvy marketers.

Value-added programs can be credited with enhancing the educational materials available to advisors, this material often being more timely than that provided by the firms themselves. Because vendors are much more focused on a particular product (their own) than brokerage firms or banks—that sell an array of products— vendors can focus on the sales support tools advisors need to sell those products. Most banks and brokerages have accepted this sales and educational support wholeheartedly. Many count on the largesse of product companies to conduct major sales and training conferences, as well as extra funding for ongoing operations.

Look for improvement in value-added programs as product companies upgrade their offerings and personalize features to fit your unique needs. The next wave of such programs more closely will match the support requirements of particular advisor types, as companies conduct more analyses of advisor practices and identify needs they can meet. The value-added support these vendors will provide are likely to fall into seven categories.

Sales ideas. Wholesalers traditionally have provided sales ideas for their featured products. The ideas typically are created by the sales or marketing departments of the product vendor, and the most valuable ideas result from product innovations or new regulatory developments, such as changes in the tax law. Also of value are ideas already tested by other advisors. Wholesalers should be able to relate specific success stories and apply the results to your practice. Challenge wholesalers to find a way to fit their products to your clientele.

Market research. Many top advisors have impressed clients by presenting the virtues of a new product or uncovering a new investment idea. The source of many of these innovations, of course, has been a vendor. The competition among product vendors and investment managers is boosting the level of market research they conduct for your benefit. Take advantage of their findings and translate the data into actionable strategies for your practice.

Seminars. The managed account business owes much of its growth to the willingness of investment managers to provide client educational seminars. The concept of hiring a discretionary manager was attractive to many advisors and clients, but meeting a representative or portfolio manager from the management firm was necessary before turning over the money. Combined with new market research or a new product need, seminars remain a very effective educational tool for top advisors. With clients anxious to learn more about investment and financial topics, a high-quality seminar program with revolving topics and speakers can be a referral bonanza. Use the manpower provided by good wholesalers with strong presentation skills to maintain a flow of new information to your clients. Do not hesitate to ask product companies to design seminars to fit your clientele or target market. Their standard *PowerPoint* presentations can be adapted to fit your needs. If you have the inclination and interest to present the program yourself, ask the product firm for the needed materials and support.

Client presentations. One of your greatest educational opportunities is to have a company representative present a new product idea to your clients. You get the chance to learn the product's features firsthand and to hear answers to common questions. Too many advisors fail to take advantage of new product innovations because they believe they must know everything about a product before attempting to present it to clients. Leverage your time and expertise by inviting the wholesaler to present directly to some "safe" clients and make your decisions based on the fit.

Technical education. Clients are attracted to advisors who they believe are on the cutting edge of innovation. Competitive pressure from other advisors is a powerful incentive for you to try new ideas before clients hear of them from someone else. For example, when Congress reduced the contributions executives could make to company pension plans, savvy marketers at leading pension consulting firms quickly devised an alternative. If you can provide technical insights into issues of real concern to your clients, your prestige will soar along with the referrals of clients anxious to work with an innovative advisor. Question your vendors about possible changes in their markets or products, and be the first advisor to inform clients of new developments.

Practice management support. Many top companies are investing in true practice management programs to aid the growth of your practice. Several of the new entries were described earlier.

Top advisors are asking for specific help in particular areas and challenging their product vendors to provide solutions. Take advantage of the companies' interest in your practice to specify your needs. Of particular interest to many advisors is information about advanced marketing tactics and customer segmentation. Other practices require data about employee hiring and compensation practices. Whatever the practice management need, there is a vendor company willing to help.

Personal coaching. Some wholesalers have the ability to help you stay focused on your business plan. Others are inexperienced or so concerned about the sales of their own products that they don't have the skills or interest to assist you. Steer clear of those wholesalers, but share your business plan with and enlist the support of those professionals who can provide true added value to your practice. Top advisors frequently talk about the impact on their success of a wholesaler who coached them during their formative years. Many product companies have boosted their efforts to reach top advisors by retaining the services of professional marketing and sales coaches. Usually, these professionals are available in group seminars, teleconferences, on audio/videotapes, or on Web sites. In some cases, vendor firms are helping to underwrite the costs of working directly with top coaches like Bill Bachrach, Steve Moeller of American Business Visions, Leo Pusateri of Pusateri Consulting and Training, and Steve Saenz of Paragon Resources. These trainers hold retreats and conferences for top advisors, as well as provide in-person, telephone, and e-mail support. Because theirs are expensive services, you should propose an incentive program to your vendors that rewards your practice's product sales with additional coaching support.

Vendor wholesalers traditionally have been known for their pizza lunches, trinkets, and product literature. Many offer much more than that. Look for true business-building support in the form of shared marketing costs, client appreciation sessions, advanced sales training, and personal coaching services. The best companies know who you are and are anxious to focus their attention in ways that can best help you do more business. Make sure you maintain a list of product vendor companies with whom you do business, as well as a tally of the assets under management at each, plus annual new sales. Report to each company the goals of your practice and solicit their advice and support. Wholesalers have the greatest incentive to support you, while their inside salespeople have the greatest availability. Make contact with a sales manager—with the support of the wholesaler—to help ensure your wholesaler's ability to keep the attention flowing.

What Jack Sharry Wants to Do for You

*J*ack Sharry is president of the Private Client Group at Phoenix Investment Partners. He started out at what is now Morgan Stanley Dean Witter and rose to national sales manager in the firm's insurance/annuity division. Jack headed broker-dealer sales and, later, retail marketing at Putnam Investments before joining Phoenix in 1995, where he is responsible for the individual investment management business.

Competing against Oppenheimer, Invesco, Furman Selz, Regent, Rittenhouse, 1838 Investment Advisors, Brandes, and other large money managers active in the individual managed accounts business, Phoenix has been active in the "value added" wholesaling concept since the mid-1990s.

"Wholesalers have been the classic hander-outer of golf balls and tickets to sports events. But that's passe," Sharry says. "We now back up our external wholesalers with internal wholesalers, whom we call Investment Consultants, and telemarketers to help the individual advisor respond more professionally to their clients. For example, we produce 5,000 asset allocation proposals a month, which we can deliver by e-mail. We're also getting to the point where we can help advisors and their clients go online and look at a proposal on their own computers at the same time. Soon we'll have audio and video as part of those presentations. We refer to that process as e-wholesaling, and we're building all sorts of tools so that advisors will be able to conduct their relationship with us and with their customers online.

"We recognize there are a gazillion Web pages out there and that everyone is flooded with information. But we feel that if we can provide the tools that help advisors solve problems, their clients will enjoy greater success and the advisor will come back to us. If we're easier to access, easier to use, and easier to rely on—assuming we continue to provide good products and good value—we will become the supplier of choice."

YOUR MOVES

With competition so keen in the marketplace for serving affluent clients, you can no longer afford to go it alone. Whether you build a formal or informal team, or seek the resources of outsiders, you must take some action to build connections between your service-providing practice and others who can support you.

Where to start? Begin by devoting one hour a week—under 3 percent of your weekly work schedule—to seeking outside links and support. Consider these activities:

- Scanning the Web sites of your existing and potential product suppliers. They post new information constantly. You can incorporate some of this information into your business immediately; other material can be filed for future use.
- Call wholesalers and vendor representatives whom you feel are more than mere product salespeople. They love to share their insights with advisors who take the time and interest to call.

- When you see the names of attorneys or accountants quoted in the local press, and their comments are particularly astute, write the expert a personal note. Being noticed is flattering, and your note will distinguish you from the crowd of other advisors the outside expert encounters.
- Volunteer. When you are involved in a favorite charity or other activity, you are bound to meet professionals—whether directly at the activity you choose or through referrals—who can help you build your business. Importantly, the allied professionals you meet this way invariably share your outlook and values, which increases the likelihood you will find yourselves trusting one another.

These steps should help in making your practice more outwardly focused. Of course, the object of all this effort is to enable you to increase your business and prosper in the battle to attract and retain affluent clients. Next, we will take a look at one of the obvious, but often unstated, challenges of the financial advice business—wresting clients from other advisors.

Chapter 5

*C*apturing Your Share of the Pie

*Your success depends on wresting
assets from other advisors; here's how
to do it.*

So far, most of our discussion has focused on ways to position yourself to serve affluent clients. We've talked about the complex financial demands of affluent business owners and how to structure your practice to meet those demands. Now let's concentrate on your business. Your challenge, if you want your business to grow, is to gather additional assets. This can be done in two ways: by attracting new assets from existing clients or by attracting new clients.

ASSET CAPTURE

We call the process of attracting additional assets from the affluent individuals who already are your clients *Asset Capture*. We know that the affluent tend to diversify their assets among several advisors—often three or four when clients have at least $1 million of investable assets. This diversification springs from several motives. First, as Dan Leemon's strategy team at Charles Schwab Company has learned through its outstanding focus-group research of the affluent, most clients simply don't feel comfortable consolidating their assets with one provider. Far from being an indictment of their trusted advisors, this tendency to diversify their holdings is seen by the wealthy as a natural protective measure. They simply don't want to put all their golden eggs in one basket. They feel it is too risky to trust one person with all or most of their wealth.

Second, as we've already seen, clients diversify advisors to seek additional expertise. The breadth of your clients' financial needs is daunting, especially to them. Since many clients doubt that a single financial advisor has the expertise to handle all their complex needs, they tend to seek the counsel of specialists. A client satisfied with your advice about investments, for example, might not look to you for advice about estate planning because they don't expect you to be an expert in that area, too. As a result, many clients choose other advisors to address roles they assume to be beyond the expertise or interest of their current advisors.

When financial services are grouped into five key categories—investments, retirement planning, estate planning, executive benefits (like stock option plans and nonqualified deferred-compensation plans), and insurance services (health, disability, long-term care)—affluent clients tend to seek out and favor specialists in each area. Time and again advisors to affluent clients find they have little success in expanding their relationships beyond the first category of services they offered. In other words, if an advisor offered estate planning advice at the start of a relationship, that's as far as the relationship progressed in most cases.

What does this mean for the advisor? It means you can expand your business by positioning yourself to get additional assets by providing the service you now provide. If you are a product or service specialist and can demonstrate the high level of performance that affluent investors demand, by all means stick with your model. Thousands of very successful advisors are specialists in one, or perhaps two, areas. But experience teaches another lesson: If you choose to expand your role to offer your existing base of clients expertise in several areas beyond your current concentration of excellence, you must work to change client perceptions of your strengths. And you must work from your existing base of clients so that your positioning makes sense. Let's explore this avenue.

You Are What Your Clients Think You Are

Back in the late 1980s a very successful broker telephoned Steve, hopping mad about a meeting he'd just held with a longtime client. During the meeting, the client had told the broker about a municipal bond unit investment trust that he had just purchased from another broker.

"What nerve!" screamed the broker, upset over the client's disloyalty. But if the client truly were being disloyal, "Why," Steve asked the broker, "did he reveal his purchase at all?" The broker kept boiling.

"That's the worst of it—he didn't understand why I got so upset. He said he saw the information in a newspaper ad."

"Well," Steve asked, "what kind of securities are in the account that you manage for the client?"

"Mutual funds and stocks," came the reply.

Steve asked when he first proposed the idea of a municipal bond unit trust to the client. There was no response. "So is it at all possible that your client is *not aware* that you sell unit trusts?" Silence again.

It's natural for clients not to understand the range of products and services you offer. Financial services are intangible and complex, and most clients don't spend a lot of time thinking about service delivery. They want expert solutions to their problems, and they'll put up with inconvenience if that's what they believe is necessary to find the perceived expertise.

Steve saw this firsthand when he was a brokerage firm executive in the 1980s. The firm he worked for grew primarily by acquisition, and as it acquired firms that served the same geographic markets, it discovered that many of its own clients had accounts with the firm that was being acquired. Curiously, most of these "duplicate" accounts bore almost no resemblance to each other. Obviously, clients were selecting advisors for the product or service expertise they believed they possessed. And after the firms were acquired, most clients retained both their brokers!

But here is the critical point: The affluent client's desire for expertise does not preempt the opportunity to cross-sell other services. Clients *demand* expertise, but they *delight* in convenience. The problem is assembling all that expertise in one place with credibility. Since it is unrealistic to expect that you can convince clients of your expertise in a broad range of financial services, it's best to start your broadening efforts among clients who know you best— your own. And the best place to start that broadening effort is with a thorough analysis of your book.

A Look at Your Book

Here's an exercise to gauge how you are perceived by your best clients and where they believe your expertise lies. Consider each of your top 20 client relationships. List client names down one column, and make a series of additional columns—five to ten, if necessary—to the right of your client list. Refer to your files and account statements and write down at the very top of each column the services you provide to these top clients. As in the worksheet shown on pages 96 and 97, these services could come under the headings of Securities, Financial Planning, Asset Allocation, Estate

Planning, Business Succession Planning, Managed Accounts, Life Insurance, and Long-Term Care Insurance.

Now, consider each client you listed. Looking across at the product and service columns, check off the services you *currently* provide to that client. Do the same for each client—all the way down the list of 20.

Do the math. Tally the checkmarks for each product/service category and compare the percentage of clients that use the service. What percentage of your top-20 clients have managed accounts? How many use you to plot asset allocation strategies? To whom do you provide estate planning or business succession planning services?

This exercise gives you a feel for your identity among your best clients. If someone were to ask one of your best clients for more information about what you do for that client, what would the client say? This is important information, because the answer reveals your client's perception of your expertise and forms the basis for potential referrals.

Many top advisors follow the spirit of this exercise by directly asking their best clients what they believe the advisor provides. This can be a valuable exercise because the future of your business may lie in the collective impression of you that exists in your clients' minds. Ironically, your own impression of your expertise is less important than what clients think. When we ask advisors about their expertise—which we frequently do—we usually get back far too general a response. Affluent clients are understandably skeptical about such claims of comprehensive expertise. As one client explained: "For an advisor to tell me they can do it all is crazy. No one can. And no smart client would expect it. I know that Sears sells clothes, but Sears' clothes aren't up to my standards. Sure, it would be nice to save some time and buy clothes when I'm there buying tools. But the bottom line is that I buy wrenches at Sears and clothes at a specialty shop."

Your Book

	Client	Securities	Financial Planning	Asset Allocation
1				
2				
3				
4				
5				
6				
7				
8				
9				
10				
11				
12				
13				
14				
15				
16				
17				
18				
19				
20				

Estate Planning	Business Succession Planning	Managed Accounts	Life Insurance	Long-Term Care Insurance	Other

A Question of Perception

*T*he questions are simple, "What do you do for your clients?" and "What does your financial advisor do for you?" Here are some of the possible responses you might receive if you asked what is essentially the same question of both interested parties:

Advisor Answers	*Client Answers*
Provide total financial solutions	Sells municipal bonds
Provide comprehensive financial planning	Gives me good investment ideas
Free clients' time by taking care of investments	Handles restricted stock sales without a hitch
Help clients preserve and increase wealth	Keeps me from making stupid mistakes
Explain and take care of asset allocation	Gets me into the right funds

Suppose that after looking over your product worksheet you see that you checked a particular product or service column more than ten times. That means you're offering that service to more than half of your top clients. Fifteen or more checks and you are definitely focusing your practice on that product or service. With that kind of dominance, the majority of your top clients probably would identify you as an authority in that area.

What if there isn't a predominance of checkmarks? Then try to understand why and how those sales occurred. Did you make a concerted effort to expand the relationship into those areas or did a client suggest the addition? Think again of what a client might say when asked by a nonclient about the services you provide. Consider how you would *like* to be perceived by your best clients. What is your niche? What do you do best? What would you like to learn more about? A natural extension to your practice may be found in a new product or service.

This exercise reveals the "holes" in your product and service array that can be targets for earning additional client assets. Examine each case and understand why one client has given you a managed account but not the estate plan, and another has consulted you for succession planning but didn't turn over the assets.

Increasing Your Share

Once you have assessed your strengths—and, more importantly, your clients' perceptions of your strengths—your goal is to increase the share of your clients' assets by providing them with those services where you are perceived to have expertise. Given that affluent clients will diversify their holdings among advisors, your goal is to earn the greatest possible share of those assets. Currently, other advisors manage assets you do not. There is no easy way to say this: *Asset Capture is all about getting the client to transfer assets from another advisor to you.* So get comfortable with the concept of constructing a battle plan. The process can be laid out in three stages: client evaluation, identifying the opportunity, and asking for the money.

ASSET CAPTURE STAGE 1: CLIENT EVALUATION

Who are the clients you will target to earn additional assets? We know from our work with advisors that the typical book or practice is dominated by a relatively small number of top clients. In most cases, the old 80:20 rule doesn't apply. Many times, as few as five top clients account for 95 percent of an advisor's business. You may have a few more. "True clients" are those who meet the criteria for a solid and mutually beneficial relationship. Try these guidelines for what makes a "true client" among your very top clients:

- Client maintains business despite market swings.
- Client adds assets systematically.
- Client is source of at least one referral per year of another UHNW client.
- Client utilizes the full range of your capabilities.
- Client makes you aware of the fact that your advice affects most of his or her assets.

Unfortunately, data we collected recently for AIM Management challenges the position taken by many advisors who claim they have at least 20 to 30 "true clients." The reason some of these high-level clients are not their "true" clients is that they don't provide the advisor with any additional assets (see Figure 5.1). The reason? They probably didn't ask their clients for more money.

The data indicate that if advisors don't ask, they don't get (see Figure 5.2). An interesting contrast to the data reveals the success of advisors who summon the courage to ask for more money.

FIGURE 5.1

The Top 50 Clients: Percent of Clients Who Added Assets in the Past Year

Assets Added	By Clients
None	49.8%
Less than 10% of clients	9.7%
10% to 25% of clients	11.5%
26% to 50% of clients	1.7%
51% to 75% of clients	7.2%
More than 75% of clients	20.1%

N=1,097 advisors

Source: AIM/Gresham, *Wealth Management Survey 2000.*

FIGURE 5.2

The Top 50 Clients: Percent of Clients Who Were Asked by Their Advisors for More Assets

Clients Asked	By Advisors
None	51.5%
1% to 24% of clients	18.4%
25% to 49% of clients	18.2%
50% to 75% of clients	11.9%
More than 75% of clients	0.0%

N=1,097 advisors

Source: AIM/Gresham, *Wealth Management Survey 2000.*

Let's look at this phenomenon in two other ways (see Figures 5.3 and 5.4).

FIGURE 5.3

Success and the Top 50 Clients: Percentage of Clients Who Were Asked by Their Advisors for More Assets

Percentage of the Advisor's Top 50 Clients Asked	Advisor's Income Under $75,000	Advisor's Income $75,000 to $300,000	Advisor's Income $300,000 and over
None	93.0%	53.2%	22.5%
1% to 24% of clients	5.2%	28.8%	18.1%
25% to 49% of clients	1.5%	13.0%	33.9%
50% to 75% of clients	0.3%	5.0%	25.5%
More than 75% of clients	0.0%	0.0%	0.0%

N=1,097 advisors

Source: AIM/Gresham, *Wealth Management Survey 2000.*

FIGURE 5.4

Success and the Top 50 Clients: Of Clients Asked for Assets,
Percentage Who Gave Them

Percent of Top 50 Clients Giving More	Advisor's Income Under $75,000	Advisor's Income $75,000 to $300,000	Advisor's Income $300,000 and over
Less than 10%	95.5%	65.3%	23.6%
10% to 25%	4.2%	31.2%	22.3%
26% to 50%	.3%	2.9%	44.1%
51% to 75%	0.0%	.6%	10.0%
More than 75%	0.0%	0.0%	0.0%

N=1,097 advisors

Source: AIM/Gresham, *Wealth Management Survey 2000.*

Note the success of the highest earning advisors, who earned additional investments from their top clients.

Now consider the third criterion of a "true client"—referrals (see Figure 5.5). Again, the survey indicates that only the top advisors earn referrals from their best clients.

As we discussed earlier, clients often go to other advisors not because they are dissatisfied with you, but because they aren't aware you offer the product or service they need or that you have expertise in that area. We were able to get some data about relative "penetration" rates of different services in the AIM/Gresham survey. We found that advisors simply are not offering a significant number of key affluent-client services. These gaps represent opportunities for anyone trying to make inroads among the affluent.

For example, when asked what services they provide to their top 50 clients, fewer than 5 percent of the advisors who responded said they provided estate-planning services. Now, recall from earlier chapters that estate planning and business succession planning were the

FIGURE 5.5

Success and the Top 50 Clients: Percentage of Top Clients Who Made a Referral in the Past Year

Percentage of Top 50 Clients Making Referrals	Advisor's Income Under $75,000	Advisor's Income $75,000 to $300,000	Advisor's Income $300,000 and over
None	95.3%	70.7%	28.2%
Less than 10%	2.8%	15.8%	9.8%
10% to 25%	1.1%	9.9%	4.4%
26% to 50%	.4%	2.7%	32.4%
51% to 75%	.4%	.9%	24.1%
More than 75% of clients	0.0%	0.0%	1.1%

N=1,097 advisors

Source: AIM/Gresham, *Wealth Management Survey 2000.*

most important concerns of affluent business owners. Nevertheless, despite the importance of estate planning, most financial advisors do not offer this service to their clients (see Figure 5.6)! And of

FIGURE 5.6

The Top 50 Clients: Percentage Provided with Estate Planning

1 to 9 clients	37.3%
10 to 19 clients	15.7%
20 to 29 clients	15.7%
30 to 39 clients	9.8%
40 to 49 clients	5.8%
All 50 clients	15.7%

N=51 advisors (4.8 percent of all advisors)

Source: AIM/Gresham, *Wealth Management Survey 2000.*

the minuscule 4.8 percent who offer estate planning, 53 percent provide it to fewer than half their top clients. I would argue that a service you provide for only 20 of your top 50 clients is probably not a strong focus—and certainly does not bode well for referrals. If fewer than half of your top clients receive a service from you, the other half is not buying for some reason. Could it be focus? Regardless of the reason, the likelihood of these clients referring another client to you for that service is very slim.

But there is more to the story. What about the top advisors—those earning $300,000 a year and more? Do they use estate planning differently? They certainly do. (See Figure 5.7.)

Clearly, focus has its rewards. The highest earning advisors offering estate-planning services provide those services to virtually all of their top 50 clients. Note also the split in the sample among the top advisors. Nearly half of the highest earning advisors providing

---

FIGURE 5.7

Success and the Top 50 Clients: Number Provided with Estate Planning for a Fee

Number of Top 50 Clients Served	Advisor's Income Under $75,000	Advisor's Income $75,000 to $300,000	Advisor's Income $300,000 and over
1 to 9 clients	40.0%	41.9%	26.7%
10 to 19 clients	20.0%	12.9%	20.0%
20 to 29 clients	20.0%	19.4%	6.7%
30 to 39 clients	0.0%	16.1%	0.0%
40 to 49 clients	0.0%	3.2%	13.3%
All 50 clients	20.0%	6.5%	33.3%

N=51 advisors (4.8% of all advisors)

Source: AIM/Gresham, *Wealth Management Survey 2000.*

estate-planning services deliver those services to almost all of their clients; another segment offers the services to a very limited number of clients. Focus is clear in both cases—or rather it is easy to see that advisors either see estate planning as a core service for all clients, or as a key service that must be available. Advisors who focus intently on estate planning deliver it to all of their clients; the other advisors have a minority of clients involved, and likely provide other key services at the same time. This data indicates two potential models for success—the specialist, who provides a key service to all clients, and the wealth manager, who delivers the service as needed to clients for whom more comprehensive advice is required.

Another example could be long-term care insurance. LTC is not widely sold among financial advisors according to our survey—exposing another opportunity to add additional assets of affluent clients and expand your control of the client's financial activity. Just 8.3 percent of all advisors provide their clients with long-term-care insurance, but even these advisors don't achieve great penetration of their top 50 clients (see Figure 5.8).

FIGURE 5.8

The Top 50 Clients: Percentage Provided with Long-Term Care Insurance

1 to 9 clients	55.0%
10 to 19 clients	23.6%
20 to 29 clients	12.4%
30 to 39 clients	3.4%
40 to 49 clients	3.4%
All 50 clients	2.2%

N=89 advisors (8.3 percent of all advisors)

Source: AIM/Gresham, *Wealth Management Survey 2000.*

Numbers Alone Don't Tell the Story

If you're like most advisors, completing the previous exercise leads to a depressing conclusion: Many of your best clients do not fit the model of a "true client" as described by our criteria. Yet our empirical benchmarks don't tell the whole story because they omit other criteria, some of which are simply common sense. The quality of your client relationships is not based on numbers alone. It can be gauged by how well you know your clients, their families, their other advisors, and their colleagues. Can you name your clients offhand? Do you know the names of their spouses, their children, and their pets? Do you know their interests? Their favorite charities? The schools and colleges that are important to them? How can you claim a great client relationship if you don't know the most important information about a client's family?

The bottom line is that you must get to know your clients very well. Good clients are hard to find. If you have them, you should make every effort to turn these good clients into great clients. Start doing that before you even attempt to go further. Many potentially solid client relationships have been destroyed by the advisor's assumption that the relationship is better than it is. Don't risk it!

ASSET CAPTURE STAGE 2:
IDENTIFYING THE OPPORTUNITY

Once you are confident that your relationships are indeed strong, and you've determined the clients from whom you may be able to attract additional assets, ask yourself the next logical question: "Why should these clients bring more assets to me?" This question raises a more problematic issue than merely whether you offer the missing product or service the client needs. It raises the specter of the client having to make a difficult decision—deciding to take money to buy *your* recommended purchase. Since the status quo and inertia are always your chief competitions, you must be sensitive to clients' feelings about other advisors and must give clients compelling reasons to make a switch.

Let's start with the most basic reasons a client might transfer additional assets to you—a missing product or service. There are many openings for a savvy advisor among the many products and services needed by affluent clients. Identify the missing services by using the grid in Figure 4.1 on page 66, which gives you and the client a single view of the client's overall financial needs. What issues haven't you tackled? How confident is the client of solutions to the many needs depicted on the chart? Where are the gaps?

In going after the "missing" products or services your client doesn't receive from you, your best chance to attract additional assets often results from the service failures of others. If someone else has dropped the service ball in some way, you can be the one to pick it up. Remembering what we know about affluent business owners, consider offering something in the area of estate planning. Business owners' primary concerns are led by a need for estate planning and business succession planning. Yet research indicates that many affluent business owners—as many as one-quarter or more—have not gotten around to executing a solid estate plan. More significant is the suggestion by estate planning professionals that an even greater number of clients have an estate plan that is out-of-date. How many estate planners keep tabs on their clients' plans and pick a date to revise those plans? This may be your area of opportunity.

Lewis Walker, CFP, CIMA, CRC, who heads Walker Capital Management in Norcross, Georgia, starts out by getting as much information about each client as possible. At the start, he inquires whether they have an estate plan, and if they do, he asks to see it. Walker, who is chairman of the Institute for Certified Investment Management Consultants and a columnist for *On Wall Street* magazine, points out that some multimillionaires don't even have wills, while others have generic wills cranked out by attorneys. Often, they believe that a generic will constitutes a complete estate plan. If Lew knows that a client has assets elsewhere—and he usually asks—he may request copies of their statements from the other firm to make sure his recommendations are balanced with the other portfolio.

To identify services you may not be delivering, talk to your clients about their array of needs and query them about their preparations for life events including disability and long-term care. Continue searching for an issue that disturbs them, that makes them feel unsettled, and that keeps them up at night. Use the Future Shock Grid in Chapter 8 to prompt discussion of these events and to start clients talking about their concerns.

ASSET CAPTURE STAGE 3: ASKING FOR THE MONEY

Let's recap. To capture additional assets from your affluent clients, first determine which of your clients have significant assets elsewhere. You probably can guess which clients fall into this category, but you may not have questioned them about the location of the assets or the reasons for the other relationships. One veteran wirehouse broker we know in Kentucky has developed a subtle, yet effective, way to discover his clients' other assets. John C. gives each client a "financial organizer"—essentially a binder that contains tabs and statements for each type of account held by the client (joint account, trust account, IRA account, estate plan, will, etc.). He asks his clients to bring the binder with them to each of their quarterly meetings for review. The effectiveness of the binder lies in its development. John inserts tabs for programs he believes the client should have—such as estate planning—even if the client is not doing anything in that area at all or is working with an advisor other than John (and John may or may not know initially whether the client is using another advisor).

John has found that in addition to inserting material he sends, many of his clients insert their own documentation into the binder, as well as material from other advisors, revealing to him the other components of their portfolio. If he observes that a particular section is empty, he asks whether the client has considered that area in his or her overall plan. This simple organizer—actually, it need not be more than a nice loose-leaf notebook with well-marked dividers and pockets—has differentiated John from other advisors. It is an extremely useful tool for the client and costs John all of about $20, yet he finds it an invaluable aid when he probes for information about the client's plan. Clients not only provide him with useful information—and often more money, when he asks—but they thank him for helping them get organized.

So now it's pretty much over, right? All you have to do is pop the question: "May I take that extra $100,000 that's been burning a hole in your pocket?" As you might expect, things don't happen that easily. Asking for money is relatively simple; having the client turn it over becomes problematic. The reason? The movement of assets to you raises several discomforting rational and emotional issues in the client. Consider what runs through the client's mind:

- Where will the funds come from?
- What will I say to the advisor who's handling the money now?
- Will I have to fire that advisor?
- Should I do something else with the money?
- What if I don't do anything?
- Even if this is the right thing to do, should I do it now?
- If I wait, what's the worst that can happen?

A Tale of the Roof

Compare the challenge of asking clients for additional assets to a tale Steve likes to call the "Story of the Good and Truthful Building Contractor." Imagine yourself the central character of our story—a homeowner who has retained a contractor to build an addition onto your house. The project is extensive, but the contractor and his team have done a great job. You are delighted because the addition was completed on time and within your specified budget (this is obviously a fable, but go with the flow). You pay the contractor and begin to enjoy the addition.

Act II. It's a Saturday morning a few weeks later and you are busy with your family. The doorbell rings. You look out the front window to see the contractor standing at your door. Your adrenaline starts to flow. Why is the contractor here? The addition's completed, the contractor's been paid—what's wrong? You open the door with some apprehension. The contractor greets you seriously and says:

"Sorry to bother you on a Saturday morning, but I wanted to make sure we got you on the calendar. By the way, thanks for the check—I wish all of our clients paid us as promptly."

"You're welcome," you reply quizzically, "what do you mean, 'put us on the calendar'?"

"Well, while we were here doing the addition, we noticed that your roof is in bad shape and really needs to be replaced. And since it is the most important part of the house—and a pretty big job for us—we wanted to make sure you were on our calendar."

"My roof needs to be replaced?" you blurt out. To say you're shocked and not exactly thrilled by that bit of news is an understatement. Yet you have no reason to doubt the contractor, since your experience with him has been very good. He's delivered everything he promised, and his professional opinions have proven to be reliable. You can't argue with him, but do you go forward? How much is this going to cost? Will your leaky "rainy day" house account cover a multi-thousand-dollar emergency? Do you feel a little guilty and stupid for not knowing the roof needs to be replaced?

Put Yourself in the Client's Place

Now switch players. This time, you're the contractor and your clients are the homeowners. Do you get a sense of how uncomfortable clients probably feel when you ask them for additional assets? Sure, you've delivered good performance over the years, and your advice is trustworthy, yet the client you've approached hadn't expected to lay out big cash to fix a leaky estate plan until you mentioned it. What's more, even if the client has the money to go along with your suggestion, until now he hadn't considered spending it on something from which he will derive little or no immediate benefit or pleasure. At least a vacation, like a house addition, improves the quality of life. But an estate plan? Sure, it's as essential as a solid roof and more important than a Caribbean cruise, but who makes a photo album of their latest estate plan?

Looking at your suggestion from the client's point of view reveals why asking clients for more assets isn't as simple as it seems. Clients already have mental pictures of how they want to use their money; your suggestion throws cold water on their dreams. The fact that what you are telling them is true and that it will be helpful to them and their families in the long run is no consolation. In fact, the value they perceive in your idea may even make them feel selfish or guilty. Procrastination can follow guilt, and then apathy.

Steve G., a financial advisor in Pennsylvania, goes so far as to say that in his dealings with prospective clients, his biggest competition is consumer spending. "Do they need another home or a better car? No. Even the most affluent clients should reduce their spending and fully protect what they have. But they don't."

OK, maybe that's what clients should be doing, but they aren't. They still experience difficulty in making rational financial decisions that don't let them enjoy the rush that comes with a big consumer purchase. The bottom line of the Asset Capture process, therefore, is that even your best clients must be walked through it. No matter how good their account performance in recent years and no matter how much they like and respect you, they will need some prepping before you challenge them about big needs like business succession planning or their estate. You don't want to be a figural contractor and show up unannounced at the doorstep of a good client, surprising him with an eminently reasonable—but costly and unplanned—expense. You need a process and a forum that enables you to discuss a client's needs so that surprise and shock are reduced, permitting your client to assimilate the emotions your suggestions will trigger. In short, you need a better meeting.

THE KEY TO ASSET CAPTURE: CLIENT MEETINGS

Advisors often tell us that they are in close contact with their clients. Our response is, "How close is close?" How many contacts represent a significant tie to a client, and would the client agree with you? As we've discussed, highly satisfied affluent clients say they are in contact with their primary financial advisor an average of 14 times in six months. That's 28 times a year. "Wow, I don't call my mother that often," exclaimed one wirehouse rep when we told him the figure. Yet most good advisors exceed the 14-contact benchmark without realizing it. Phone calls, social visits, personalized mailings, and e-mails all can be valued components of a contact plan. Unfortunately, not all advisors are in sufficient contact with their best clients. Advisors who do contact their clients regularly reap the rewards of that attention.

In a survey of financial advisors we conducted in the summer of 2000 for AIM Management, we found that the highest-earning advisors—those making over $300,000 of income (not gross commissions or fees) per year—regularly have in-person meetings with their best clients. In fact, 76 percent of the survey respondents earning $300,000 or more reported that they met with each of their top 50 clients three or more times in the past year.

The movement to fees helps reinforce the regularity of advisor-client meetings—in a way. While separate managed accounts and their associated performance reports tend to reinforce the idea of quarterly review meetings, the meetings seem to be a case of the tail wagging the dog. Think about it for a moment. A client with a managed account receives a statement for the year's first quarter probably sometime early in May—at about the same time the client's April month-end account statement arrives. That's hardly prompt reporting by today's standards. Worse, *all* your clients with managed accounts are receiving their statements. You now face a crush of explaining many less-than-timely reports in a few weeks at most. How will you manage your time? An even more compelling question: Do you want to focus your conversation on the account's quarterly performance? If the account has increased in value, you can't really claim credit or brag about your choice of managers because (a) the performance wasn't your doing, and (b) you sold the client on the concept of a separately managed account because you stressed long-term results, not quarterly performance. So what if it's up for the quarter? It's good news that you're reviewing, but what else can you say?

If the account has declined in value, on the other hand, the fall-off is not your fault. At the same time, you can't dodge the responsibility bullet nor ignore the fact, neither. This frustrating scenario repeats itself every quarter at every brokerage office across the country. What do you say? When do you say it? And how do you change the script? It's time for the client review meeting to use a new template: the business meeting model.

Before Your New-Style Meeting

A good business meeting has a structure. And that's what you should bring to your client meetings from now on. Structure your sessions with clients as you would a formal business meeting. Since most affluent clients are businesspeople, they reward efficiency because they appreciate people who save them time. To put a time-saving, effective structure into place, think about the meeting's basics: the what, where, how, when, and why of it.

What. What will you discuss with the client? A business meeting typically features a written agenda. An advisor we know in Ottawa sends an agenda to his top clients in advance of the meeting—typically via fax. He then solicits the client's approval as well as additions or other changes to the agenda.

Where. Consider the meeting's location. Where is it most convenient for you or the client to meet? Perhaps more importantly, how do you decide where to meet? We know a top advisor in

Boston who meets with most of his clients at their places of business. It's good that he does, because his downtown office is very cluttered and features a wall of large three-ring binders containing his clients' account statements. You get the feeling when you walk into his office that the guy does business with everyone in the Boston phone book. The broker prefers to meet with clients at their places of business because it keeps him tuned into their world and removes the potential for distractions during their meetings.

As we've seen, Steve H., a wirehouse advisor in Boston, and a top managed-account consultant, also conducts client meetings at the clients' places of business. He travels to clients because he says they don't expect it—and are very impressed and satisfied when he schedules their regular meetings.

How and when. How long should meetings last and when should you hold them? George K., our Midwest advisor who carefully culled his best clients, expects his top 30 client families to spend a full day with him at least once a year. Is that too much? It depends. Our work with top advisors indicates that three 90-minute meetings per year work best. And how much of that time should be devoted to discussing products and investment performance? One advisor we know answers bluntly: "About 15 minutes!" He fills the meeting with what he calls "the important stuff"—family concerns, the state of their business, and other matters that concern them deeply. A well-known international private banking firm used to take its best clients on an overseas trip at least once a year. While the main reason for the meeting was to learn more about key investing topics and the outlook for markets around the world, the most commonly discussed topic among the participants was their families. Think about the meeting's length from the client's point of view: If you haven't had a deep discussion in three or four months, there's a lot of ground to cover in an hour and a half.

Why. The final issue to consider as you prepare for your meeting is its goal. What do you want to happen as a result of getting together with your client? Many advisors who limit their discussion to a review of quarterly performance simply want the meeting to be over. But if a client is willing to place his trust in you as an advisor, you should have a plan for the meeting that reflects your confidence in your ability to add value. While every meeting is a challenge to defend your added value, it also provides an opportunity to prove why you deserve ongoing support and additional assets. In advance of the meeting, think about the potential, unmet needs of your client. Refer to the diagram of client needs in Chapter 4. What areas have you already reviewed with your client? Which areas require attention?

At the Meeting

If you have ever served in a formal group—a board of directors, for instance, or a community or charity organization—you are familiar with the challenge of prioritizing action steps. Many groups use Robert's Rules of Order to add structure to meetings; you can, too. Start with an agenda. By working from a written agenda, whether shared with the client in advance or not, you set the stage. Remember the old saw about eliminating meetings by requiring written agendas in advance? It's a good strategy. But we don't want to eliminate the meeting, just impose order and control. An agenda is a good way to establish who is in charge. Here's what your agenda should include:

- Minutes of the last meeting
- Old business
- "Committee" reports
- New business
- Setting priorities
- Developing action steps
- Setting the date of the next meeting
- Adjournment

Minutes of the last meeting. Sound too formal? The truth is, most of the steps can be done casually, and most segue fluidly into one another. Reviewing minutes of the last meeting has a number of benefits. First, it demonstrates to the client that you know what you both discussed at the last meeting. This by itself should be impressive, but it's also important in establishing a baseline of discussion for the current meeting. If you meet just three or four times a year for an in-depth discussion with your client, at least three and as much as four months have elapsed since you last met. It's quite likely the client forgot what you discussed at the last meeting.

Old business. After reviewing the past meeting, move on to "old business." What were the key issues remaining on the table from the last discussion? What has transpired since then? Were you supposed to do something for the client as a result of that meeting? Did you do it? This is the perfect venue in which to remind your client of the services you provide. By using a professional process with a written agenda, you are describing your ongoing services and added value—without being boastful or obnoxious. Even more important may be the chance to review any responsibilities the client had from the last meeting. Did these tasks get completed?

Committee reports. Now that you've reviewed the minutes— which shows your professional memory and command of the situation—and you've discussed actions taken by you and your client, you're ready for the "committee" reports. One advisor leads into this discussion by saying, "Let's see what our hired hands have done for us lately." Notice the emphasis on the word "us" in that sentence. This is no time to be defensive about a product or an account manager. You provided a professional recommendation that was approved by the client, and there are no guarantees. Today's affluent clients often want to be involved in the big decisions, but avoid the details. Take advantage of that interest and include them in the process. But don't shirk from discussing the alternatives in a rational way.

Committee reports can be managed-account quarterly reports and regular account statements. These documents must be related to the style, interest, and financial goals of the client. The guiding thought should be something akin to, "Here's what ABC Management has done; let's talk about what it means to you." Even a spate of temporarily bad performance has its place if there is a potential contribution. Review again why you both agreed to this investment in the first place. After the review, are there any actions you should take? For example, if a particular fund has underperformed, should you investigate potential replacements? What are you looking for and why? When will you complete your research and get back to the client? Is there any task for the client to assume?

New business. The best way to tackle the "new business" section of the agenda is to review again the multibox diagram in Chapter 4. Which issues concern the client today? What has changed since the last meeting? Engage the client, because at this stage the client may decide to withdraw either physically or emotionally, and that will short-circuit the meeting. If your goal is to use the meeting to earn additional assets, you must uncover more information.

At this point, try a technique used by many savvy advisors who want to head off having their clients say "everything's fine" and mentally begin to leave the premises. Since you can't X-ray the client to discover hidden needs, you can tell the story of another client who experienced a difficult financial event and draw the link. The client will make the connection. Here's a story Steve tried during an assignment to help advisors and their top clients focus on elder care and the need for long-term care insurance:

> Many people like you have aging parents, and few of them have considered the potential impact of their parents on their own retirement years. A couple I know who are now in their 50s had been successful executives for many years and purchased a substantial tract of land near a ski resort in Sun Valley, Idaho, several years ago. Having enjoyed the resort for

many years, the couple planned to replace their modest home with a 10,000-square-foot dream house upon their retirement, which they planned to begin very soon. At about the time retirement rolled around, the couple was forced to put their dream property up for sale. The problem? The husband's parents, who lived in Michigan, had become unable to care for themselves. Idaho was too far away to make frequent trips possible, and there was no long-term care facility in the Sun Valley area that was acceptable; so the dream died.

Situations like this are very effective in illustrating issues that clients have not thought about. The downside is that you may hit on a topic that no one wants to discuss. Unfortunately, that's the job of a valued advisor. In the same vein, another tactic for probing new business issues is the Future Shock Grid shown in Chapter 8, which reveals when age-related family issues—elder care, retirement, college—will emerge.

Priorities and action steps. To set priorities and develop action steps, focus on just a few items. Overwhelming the client with too many holes in their financial plan can backfire. Since you want to show clients the light at the end of the tunnel—not scare them in the dark—pick one or two important issues from any unfinished old business, plus one or two issues from the new business items. Confirm the importance of these issues with the client and determine a time line for completion. Your action steps might look something like this:

- Old business: Discuss the performance of ABC Value Fund.
- Action: Advisor to review alternatives to present to client by November 10.
- New business: Charitable gift.
- Priorities/Action steps: Client to consider final recipient, amount, funding source. Advisor to recommend a low-basis investment.

The next meeting. Want a great way to approach setting up your next regular client meeting? Follow the lead of a great dental practice located, coincidentally, near the headquarters of a major mutual fund company. Contrary to its languid name, The Gentle Dentist is relentless in its system for generating repeat business from difficult clients. Everyone knows that having a hygienist perform a dental cleaning every six months is a must, but most patients of The Gentle Dentist are busy executives and salespeople who routinely forget their dental appointments. The practice responded to the broken appointments by demanding that each patient fill out two reminder cards after every visit. One is sent to the patient's office and the other to the patient's home. Since both cards are hand-addressed by the patient, someone at home or at work is likely to take notice and make sure the appointment is put on a calendar. That's an effective program. Similarly, George K., our advisor in the Midwest, admonishes his top 30 client families that if they can't make their regularly scheduled meetings, he may not be able to continue working with them. He wants to see a commitment to the process. Formally setting the date of your next meeting is an important step that shows clients you care. Don't hesitate to schedule a date way out on the calendar to ensure the continuity of the process as well as the momentum.

Adjournment. Finally, formal meetings usually include a vote to adjourn in order to assure that everyone has had a chance to have their say. You should extend the same courtesy to clients. Failure to do so risks alienating them as well as ruining your chances to get more assets. Clients may not have seen you for three or four months, and they likely have spent an hour or two talking about deeply felt issues they haven't discussed with anyone in a long time. This process may have warmed them up to the point where they feel comfortable telling you about *The Other Advisor* who has $500,000 of their money and is not paying attention to them. Your client may want you to have that money, and now that you demonstrated your value and your concern they are ready and willing to move the money in your direction. Then you blow it all by saying: "I'm so glad you came in today; I'm sorry, but I have to run off to another meeting." Clunk. Opportunity lost.

Give clients time to get their ideas formulated and suggest several soft closes for the meeting—for example, by announcing the expected time of the meeting's completion at its start, and then a "gut check" about halfway through to make sure you're still respecting their time. If things are running smoothly, don't rush and don't cap your time.

Remember George K.'s all-day meetings? What's your rush? If relationships are what this business is all about, your in-depth client meetings are the nectar of your relationships—don't chug them down. The paperwork can wait. And if you're scheduling a few meetings a day, give yourself at least an hour between each one. You need time to let the unexpected happen. Let every meeting end only when it is clear that the client has put all the cards on the table and has agreed with you that there is nothing left to discuss. Probe for additional information at the close, like feedback about the meeting itself—"Did we accomplish what you hoped we would today?" "What were your expectations when you arrived this morning for our meeting?" "How did we do?" or even "Is there anything else you want to tell me that would help me to help you?"

Winning Tactic

*Family talk isn't idle chatter. Often, advisors assume that conversations about family—Where is your son planning to go to college? How are your daughter's driving lessons coming? How's your ailing mother?—are preludes to discussions about serious matters. Many times, family **is** the serious matter. Over the years, private bankers have learned one thing from the exclusive meetings they set up for their superwealthy clients at posh international resorts: The most common discussion subject among attendees is their children.*

YOU CAN'T WIN 'EM ALL

Sometimes the best plans, the best execution of those plans, and the best intentions are for naught. In dealing with clients, you sometimes come to the realization that the client doesn't need your advice, doesn't want your advice, or is such a poor fit with you intellectually, emotionally, or in his or her expectations, that your advice just won't work. At times like these—and with clients who don't deserve your attention—it makes perfect sense to throw in the towel and give up on such clients. Most advisors, of course, won't go down without a fight. In fact, essentially hopeless clients are often those who consume much of an advisor's time and energy.

Steve had an eye-opening sales experience while he was in college that involved walking away from a client, and it has stayed with him since. Here's the story, in his words:

> I worked part of one summer for Electrolux, selling high-priced vacuum cleaners door-to-door. The job was suggested by George Ball, then president of E.F. Hutton & Company, who had very kindly responded to a letter I wrote as a freshman asking for advice about how to enter the securities industry. He suggested a sales job, but not in securities or finance. He said I should first sell something I believed in. So, after asking around, the high-end Electrolux vacuum seemed to fit the bill. At over $400 in 1979, the top-of-the-line model was an expensive item. And with a 25 percent commission, it meant real money to the salesman. It would be good preparation for the investment business, I thought.
>
> The story that changed my view of selling was not related to the trials of cold calls and slammed doors. It was not about the dog bites or kid bites I endured that hot summer pushing my grocery cart around (I didn't have a car), or even the challenges of getting into some very expensive homes. Good experiences all, they weren't the key one that led to my sense of value and the need to withdraw if the client or prospect doesn't value what you do.

I was leading the office in appointments but had only average sales. I could get in any door, but I wasn't closing deals at the same pace. The sales manager—who had 20 years of experience—said he wanted to go along with me to "observe." I now know that means something else, but then I was a kid. Sales manager Tony and I went to an average home in the area, and I was able to get us in for a demonstration of the machine. In those days, the big selling technique for an Electrolux was to prove the power of the machine by running it over an area that was cleaned by the family's current vacuum, which I used first. There was a neat demonstrator bag that could be removed after using the Electrolux. The drill was to then set the bag on a clean surface and proceed to shake the dust into a neat pile, emphasizing how much dirt had been left behind by the homeowner's machine. When the horrified prospects saw the dirt left behind, they'd pony up for the Electrolux. That was the plan, anyway.

So Tony and I walked through the presentation. I did the vacuuming and the shaking while he did the talking. I ran the machine over a velvet armchair and grabbed a ton of dust that I was able to shake into three or four piles. I was delighted. Here was the proof that our prospect needed a new machine.

"Wow," said Tony to the homeowner, "That is a significant amount of dust. I think you can see the value presented by our machine."

I certainly did, but the lady just shrugged her shoulders. No reaction, no commitment, no jumping to buy—no nothing. I was about to launch into my description of the vacuum's other key features and payment plans, but Tony interrupted me with a curt but polite, "thankyouverymuchforyourtime" to our prospect. He packed up the machine in record time and was out the door before I could react. I bid my farewell to the housewife and joined him outside in the car.

"What happened?" I gasped, "Why didn't we try to sell her? She needed our machine! Didn't you see all the dirt I got out of that chair?"

"Steve," Tony said with a very calm expression, "We didn't leave because she doesn't need what we have, we left because she doesn't value what we have. Twenty years at this job has taught me not to waste my time trying to convince someone who doesn't value my services. I could be using that time to help—and sell—someone else!"

Lesson painful; lesson learned.

Your time is valuable. Good clients know that and support you accordingly. You should recognize that too. Avoid people who abuse your time. Eliminate marginal clients who don't value your time or your advice. Concentrate your time on finding and keeping good clients who make all your efforts worthwhile.

Gather More Assets Action Checklist

1. **Assess your strengths.** What's your area of expertise? Where do you excel? What do you like doing? What gives you the most satisfaction?

2. **Have your clients assess your strengths.** In what area or areas do they believe your expertise lies? What do you do for them that they really appreciate? What do they count on you for?

3. **Assess your clients.** What are they buying from you? Based on what you know about them, what are their other needs? Where do you think you could add value?

4. **Concentrate on the right clients.** Which clients do you think will be most willing to expand their relationship with you? Which clients do you most like to deal with? Who do you think has the most potential to add to your assets or to refer you to clients like themselves?

5. **Plan for more in-depth meetings.** Start formatting longer meetings now. Start scheduling client meetings further in advance. Tape your first in-depth meeting, critique it, and create a model you can follow in subsequent client meetings.

6. **Implement the meeting's outcome.** Review your meeting notes and immediately start taking the action steps that have come out of it. Create tickler files so that when you see relevant news items or other interesting material between meetings, you can send them to clients.

Chapter 6

*F*inding the Tools You Need

Technology won't eliminate your job;
it will dramatically change the way
you do business.

The pace of technological change in financial services is now so rapid and the innovations so dramatic that we tend to forget that the industry has been shaped by technology for most of its history. For example, it was a breakthrough technology of the 19th century—the telegraph—that made possible the creation of national brokerage firms. Now linked by satellite and strands of glass, we still refer to the nation's largest retail firms as wirehouses because of a long-gone communications method.

THE GROWTH OF TECHNOLOGY

Forty years ago, technology in the form of mainframe computers made possible the growth of institutional investing. Without computers, the recordkeeping functions associated with trading more than a few million shares a day would be impossible.

The Internet is the latest wave of technology to shape financial services, and its impact is just beginning to change core functions of the industry. One of the first Net phenomena, of course, was online brokerage, which married the transaction-only offering of discount brokerage with the convenience and speed of personal computers. As online firms grew in the mid-1990s, brokers' attitudes toward the new channel kept shifting. At first, the new entrants went unnoticed. Much like the nonreaction to discount brokerage two decades earlier, most traditional brokers and advisors were unaware of the new channel. Among those brokerages and advisors who noticed the arrival of E*Trade and Schwab's introduction of online services, few considered the entrants much more than curiosities that would attract a limited, high-tech following.

But as the popularity of online brokerage grew, brokers' reactions shifted from indifference to curiosity to disbelief. How could this be happening? How could so many clients be trading by themselves (and at so low a price)? Then disbelief turned to anger and resentment and fear. The wirehouses dug in their corporate heels and sneered that they would never allow their customers to trade online without the benefit of advice. In 1998, John "Launny" Steffens, who headed Merrill Lynch's retail business at the time, was quoted in the press as saying that online trading was a "serious threat to Americans' financial lives."

Of course, we all know what has happened since then. There are now more than 12 million online brokerage accounts, containing assets of roughly $1 trillion, up from $27.7 billion in 1995. The Internet is where as much as half of all retail transactions may be taking place. The truth is, it's now almost impossible to track the source of retail trading because virtually all traditional firms—including Steffens' Merrill Lynch—now enable their clients to trade over the Net. Financial advisors have gone from being threatened by the ubiquity of online trading to seeing it as a way to off-load less productive clients and trade up to those who want real advice and guidance, not merely a transaction.

THE FUTURE OF FINANCIAL TECHNOLOGY

The future course of the Internet and financial advice is likely to track the arc of online brokerage. Simply, this means that new software and technological advances probably will be ignored at first, then scorned as too radical by current leaders. The new competitors will gain market share until the deep-pocketed market leaders co-opt the new technology and use it to cement their dominance.

As an example of a technology whose time is coming, consider electronic signatures. Until recently, information about opening a new account, for instance, could be passed along electronically by phone, fax, or e-mail. Electronics ended and paper started when a client had to sign a piece of paper and send it back to an advisor in order to conduct a transaction or consent to a business agreement. No longer. The Electronic Signatures in Global and National Commerce Act, the so-called e-signature bill, has been effective since October 1, 2000. It makes the use of a digital signature as legally valid as a traditional signature written in ink on paper. Why aren't e-signatures more widely used? Blame it on the technology lag. Experts say the legality of e-signatures will have to be tested in the courts before everyone becomes comfortable with it, and as yet there are questions about the method of securing the signatures. Routine use is not expected for several years. But when that day comes, e-signatures will change the pace of financial transactions and relationships by speeding the process immeasurably and reducing the expense of creating, recording, and storing paper.

This is not the only change that's coming. Clearly, the continued acceptance of technology-based solutions and the outpouring of new Net-based financial tools and services will have serious implications for advisors.

More Net access. The number of U.S. households with Internet access is expected to grow to about 107 million by 2003, according to a study by Cerulli Associates, Inc., of Boston. Tools such as Palm Pilots, advanced cell phones, and other devices will make wireless Web access more common. People will come to expect virtually instantaneous access to information.

More self-directed investors. The pool of self-directed investors will grow, as new tools empower investors who are inclined to make their own decisions. No matter how much financial advisors pooh-pooh the quality of online advice and data, investors who are psychologically suited to handle their own investments will be happier than ever with the low-cost choices coming their way—even if it's for only part of their wealth. Cerulli finds that the self-directed are either "best-of-breed" shoppers, who seek out the best providers of a product or service in each category, or a smaller "one-stop" group who like the ease of filling all their needs at one place. Tiburon Strategic Advisors, of Tiburon, Calif., expects these online advice models to explode, with firms such as MyCFO, Morgan Online, One Harbor, Asset Planner, Direct Advice, Financial Engines, M Power, Morningstar Clear Future, and Quicken's 401(k) Advisor among the prominent providers.

More demand for occasional advice. There will be a growing number of affluent individuals who will prefer to handle much of their financial affairs online by themselves—but who still will want to consult with a financial professional occasionally for personal advice. A poll by Alliance Capital and Harris in 1999 found that the largest trade that investors are comfortable making online without advice is worth $4,500. In fact, the majority of Americans—57 percent, according to the poll—say they expect to seek financial advice from an advisor in the future, regardless of whether they trade online. These individuals will be familiar with online services and will require their advisors to work with them using the new tools. This vast "middle" market is being attacked by both Schwab and

Merrill with similar strategies—staffing giant call centers with salaried, registered advisors who are available to answer investor inquiries and provide limited advice.

Demand for Net-savvy advisors among clients who seek assistance. Clients who don't have the time or desire to do-it-themselves on the Net will expect their advisors to be accomplished masters of the latest software—or have access to those who are. Even investors who are not familiar with technology and don't wish to use it themselves now assume that most wealth management questions can be answered by a smart advisor using the right electronic tools. You will be required to be that tech- and Net-savvy advisor in order to retain and expand your business.

Are advisors using the new tools right now? Not to any great extent. Tiburon asked independent advisors about their Web use and learned the following:

- 79 percent used the Web to access investment research.
- 73 percent used it for e-mailing clients.
- 40 percent used it as a marketing tool.

For tasks that the Net handles efficiently and are not particularly finance-related, advisors were taking surprisingly little advantage of technology:

- 34 percent use the Net to download forms.
- 18 percent order supplies.
- 12 percent communicate within their offices.
- 11 percent download account information.

Since advisors typically don't spend more than a small fraction of their workday speaking with clients, ignoring the management efficiencies that the new technology brings is unfortunate.

WHAT TO DO NOW

Most advisors realize they must become more technologically adept. At the same time, they also understand the limits and frustrations of technology: Software designed for a general audience won't solve your specific needs. Programs that are supposed to work together don't. Data arrives in different formats from different vendors and must be reentered and extensively massaged in order to be useful. And everything costs at least twice as much and takes twice as long to work as the tech people say it will—that is, when you can find a tech person you understand. Evan has received so many jargon-filled press releases announcing "total solutions" that he wonders whether any tech company is even capable of explaining in plain English what its stuff does.

And what does all that "stuff" do? Rather than list the ever-changing roster of products and services offered to advisors, it may be more helpful to identify some of the areas in which technological tools are being offered.

Investments. The Internet is powering the creation of new products as well as permitting a wider distribution of products that until now have been available only through one channel or a limited number of providers. For example, advisors now can get information on hedge funds from sites including Altvest.com and Hedgeworld .com. They can have access to private equity deals and information about private equity from sites such as Prima Capital, Offroad.com, EarlyBirdCapital.com, and Garage.com. They can offer an automated 401(k) plan with investments directed to a variety of resources from ExpertPlan.com. Or they can offer an investment "basket"—which, in effect, is a separately managed account that is self-managed—from FOLIOfn. The firm recently created FOLIO Advisor, which enables an advisor to be the manager of a client's basket portfolio.

Marketing support. Contact management software such as Broker's Ally, Broker's Notebook, Gorilla for Windows from Bill Good

Marketing, and ACT! are becoming customer relationship management (CRM) tools that help advisors create and maintain a database of their clients. Other CRM products—such as ClientXchange, Junxure, and Peak 98—provide additional functionality. For advisors who want to use their Web site as a marketing vehicle, Advisor-Sites and Advisor Square are two firms that specialize in creating and maintaining Web sites for advisors. Product providers, including fund companies and asset managers, provide a wealth of calculators and customizable product data on their Web sites.

Portfolio management. All the work of asset allocation, portfolio construction, analysis, management, monitoring, and reporting can be done with the help of tools available online or as software. Scores of companies provide tools in this area, including Advent, Advisor Software, Captools, Cheshire Software, Financial Computer Support, Ibbotson, Morningstar, Performance Technologies, and Techfi.

Financial, estate, tax, and retirement planning. Many providers offer software and online services to create and assess plans in all these areas. Many of the programs include complex analytics and simulations that would be impossible to perform any other way. In this arena, providers include EISI, FinanceWare, Financial Profiles, IFDS Enterprises, Lifegoals.Com, Lumen Systems, Mobius/Checkfree, MoneyStar, Money Tree Software, and Spectra Securities Software.

Administrative and compliance support. If you feel buried in paperwork or worried that you may not be complying with your regulatory requirements, consider technical help from companies such as Amicus, BOAsoft, Financial Planning Consultants, GBS, InsMark, and National Regulatory Services. New tools that combine administrative and other functions are becoming available, too; ADVISORport.com provides an online platform that integrates portfolio construction, investment and manager selection, reporting, and administrative functions.

The lavish technology budgets of Wall Street's giant firms are evidence of the pressure on industry leaders to remain competitive. The spending also indicates the firms' need to increase efficiency and reduce dependence on costly personnel. At smaller firms and among independent planners and advisors, technology can be particularly helpful in reducing costs. Accounting firm Moss Adams, in a report it conducted for the Financial Planning Association entitled "The 2000 FPA Financial Performance & Compensation Study of Financial Planning Practitioners," found that at the average planning firm overhead expenses ate up 42.4 percent of revenues. As planning firms grow, the report found, the average revenue per principal falls—from revenues of $546,116 for a single principal to $385,678 per principal in a three-person practice. The report's authors said that if practitioners could improve their productivity by leveraging technology, they could better serve their clients and improve efficiency.

How One Advisor Went Paperless

*D*oes being a virtually all-digital practice improve efficiency? Sharon Keyfetz believes it does. She and her husband Loren are the principals of Personal Financial Consultants, Inc., and Personal Financial Consultants Securities Corporation, financial planning firms in San Ramon, Calif., <www.pfcsc.com>. Active in East Bay financial planner groups, the two CFPs (he is also a Chartered Life Underwriter and a Chartered Financial Consultant) decided in 1998 that their 425-client practice needed more efficiency.

Sharon investigated keeping digital records of all the firm's records and decided to go ahead with the idea. It involved hiring two people for nine months to scan 20 years' worth of client paperwork—the entire paper trail of their business. It also involved making sure the firm had sufficient computing power, storage media (disk drive capacity and optical storage facilities), scanners, and document imaging software (some of the providers are Laserfiche by Compulink, OnBase by Hyland Software, and DocSTAR by BitWise). The costs came to about $15,000. The costs of hardware, software, and people for an operation of a few hundred employees probably are less than $25,000, she says, and the costs are dropping as scanners and other equipment become less expensive.

Keyfetz also made certain the National Association of Securities Dealers' regulatory arm approved the move. She sent letters notifying them that the firm was switching to optical storage and that it was relying on Rule 17a-4(f) to meet its record retention requirements. She stresses, too, that digital retention is safe, pointing to several backup storage media stored in different locations. It's also secure, with access blocked by several layers of encryption and multiple passwords.

"You don't need to consider a paperless office unless you deal with large amounts of paper, you work within a regulatory framework (the NASD or SEC, for example), you need to be able to produce historical information periodically, or you must keep documents for legal purposes," Keyfetz said. "In other words, every financial professional should be interested."

While eliminating paper doesn't eliminate every practice problem, it has saved Keyfetz's firm thousands of dollars. It went from 12 large filing cabinets to two—one of which is for computer instruction manuals. The firm then moved from a 1,600-square-foot office to a 700-square-foot space, and plans to move to a cubicle in an office suite when the current lease expires. Employee hours have dropped from 100 per week to 50. The firm employs a part-time (30-hour per week) office manager and a 20-hour per week person who scans new paperwork. The firm spends about $1,000 a year on software maintenance, while it estimates it saves about $24,000 in overhead.

"In addition to the savings, going digital is the ultimate value-added service for clients. We can access their records from anyplace anytime, and give them exactly what they need. One of our clients called recently because he had lost important documents he needed to establish a tax basis. We found them in a few minutes. That made us look like heroes. Don't forget, people get divorced, they open and close businesses, they move—they just lose things. Now we have a service that let's us be extremely high tech and high touch."

Keyfetz is so keen on paperless recordkeeping that she has put information about the process on her firm's Web site and schedules speaking engagements across the country to industry groups in which she advocates the switch. She would do the talks for free, she says, but decided to charge for them to emphasize the importance of conversion. (She donates the speaking money to her favorite charities, which makes her especially enthusiastic about the digital movement.)

Despite the advantage of optical digital storage, Keyfetz estimates that fewer than a dozen firms have made the switch so far. It's not so much the cost, but the mindset, she says. And that's bound to change.

Technology Checklist

Since technology will provide you with the tools you need to grow your business, you must be willing to make continual investments of time and money in technology. Yet mastering technology, or at least staying on top of it, requires information. To gather that information, you might try the following:

- **Read** the financial planning, brokerage, insurance, and banking trade publications. They all cover technology on a regular basis and report on new products, as well as advisors who are using technology successfully. Many of the magazines also include technology information on their Web sites. FPOnline <www.fponline.com> from *Financial Planning,* for instance, conducts regular chat sessions on technology.

- **Attend trade shows.** The Financial Planning Association, Investment Management Consultants Association, and the Institute for Certified Investment Management Consultants, among others, all attract exhibitors looking to reach you. Visit the exhibit booths and find out, in person, what the services are and what they can do for you.

- **Form a technology roundtable.** Assemble a group of five to eight noncompeting advisors who are interested in sharing ideas and details of their technology experience. You should meet once or twice a year in person—perhaps in conjunction with an industry event—and talk on the phone formally every 30 or 60 days. Discuss your experiences with specific software, talk prices and performance, review ease of use, and be open about your triumphs and mistakes.

- **Check references.** Make sure to ask vendors and suppliers for names of users before you purchase any hardware or software. They'll select satisfied users, of course, but the discussion will help you better determine whether the choice you're making is the right one for you.

Chapter 7

*B*est Practices from Top Wealth Advisors

Put into your practice what today's top advisors are doing now.

Throughout our discussions, we've driven home our points by citing the experiences of some of today's most innovative advisors. We spoke to many advisors in the course of preparing this book, and we thought you might like to hear about their current business strategies. How are they attacking the affluent market? What do they think of competition and technology? How have they organized their practices to deal with clients going forward?

Here are their experiences and insights in their words. We believe that many of their practices can be applied successfully to your own business.

FUNDING RETIREMENT

Dave L.
President, independent advisory firm
Ventura, California

"I spent 30 years in retail merchandising operations and, later, franchising, before becoming a financial professional in 1993. Even with my experience, it was difficult getting clients at first, but I was used to hard work and I just put in the time and did it. Today, I manage about $50 million for 200 households. About 80 percent of my new business since 1999 is fee-based, and while I've converted only one client from commission to fees, I think a few more will convert soon. I'll give a discount to any long-term client who converts.

"About 85 percent of my current business involves retirement planning and mutual funds. For each client, I put together a 2- to 3-inch-thick binder that contains a specific outline of what I plan to do for them, how I'm going to do it, the results of a Frontier Analytics financial plan, and my specific proposals for defining asset classes and the allocation process. I also include prospectuses for all the funds I've recommended. The binder is personalized with the client's name on the front on a brass plate. Clients love it when they get this binder; they refer to it on an ongoing basis.

"I try to reach clients two to three years before they retire. I do that through seminars and referrals, and I work with two large companies who have offered early retirement packages to their employees. I plant the seed that I am an expert in retirement planning and hope they come to me when they decide they need help. Very often, they do.

"Since I had been preparing my clients for a market downturn since 1996, we handled the market drop in 2000 quite well. I received only five calls from clients during the turmoil expressing concern about what to do next. One client noted the decline on his 2000 statement and said, in effect, 'well, what can you expect?' This is the type of client you want.

"About one-third of my clients live outside my immediate area, which means I don't meet with them very often. But I do try to see everyone once or twice a year, and I send my retirement newsletters to them regularly. I see some of my more 'nervous' clients more frequently, but we don't always discuss the specifics of their account when we meet. Just meeting with them and reinforcing that they are getting the care and attention of someone who cares about their future seems to calm them down and allay their fears.

"I have an attorney to whom I refer estate planning business, and I also refer clients to a mortgage broker. But neither of these relationships involves revenue sharing."

SHE WHO SEES THE TREND BEFORE OTHERS, REAPS THE REWARDS

Lori Van Dusen, CIMA
Senior Vice President Investments, Consulting Group Director
Salomon Smith Barney
Rochester, New York

Lori got started at Shearson about 16 years ago, and we've followed her success for many years, as has our colleague, Leo Pusateri of Pusateri Consulting and Training. Lori started out thinking as a broker but ultimately decided this was not the way she wanted to build a business; she didn't want to "broker" anything. She wanted to structure a business focusing on the high-net-worth individual as well as institutions. Lori has always viewed herself as a problem solver and an integrator. Because one of the keys to a successful business is the integration of many services, she began learning about estate planning 15 years ago by working with an estate planning attorney and insurance specialist.

Since estate planning as a specialty was practically unheard of at the time, Lori quickly realized that she was perfectly positioned to become visible to a highly qualified audience. As she began to understand the entire range of tax, investment, and estate planning issues, she began to conduct seminars on those topics and built her business based on it. Who was doing this in the late 1980s? Very few. Who was doing integrative reporting? Even fewer. Although preparing the reports was a tedious manual process—especially tracking outside assets—it gave her a big head start. Lori's earlier sales experience at Xerox also helped her understand the significance of approaching clients based on situation, implication, and need.

Today, Lori has big clients, typically with about $10 million of assets, although the range extends from $5 million to $300 million. Her business-owner clients have liquefied. Most of her clients are first generation high net worth (HNW), but some are second and third generation. She runs a consulting franchise within a traditional brokerage firm, along with a partner she's had for 11 years.

What makes Lori unique? She says it's her ability to engender trust and build relationships. Her clients seek her advice and assistance in many ways: finding a job, leasing a plane, managing a portfolio. She sees these "extra" tasks as part of her job.

What about that 2000 market? Did her relationships hold up? "The year 2000 was good for my clients in one sense—it injected a dose of reality. Alternative investments helped, as did asset allocation and a few superior individual investment manager returns. None of our clients had a negative return.

"HNW clients do not want to lose any money. They want to grow their assets moderately. Dumb money was made prior to 2000. It was a great year to test downside risk. The last thing the HNW clients want to hear is that they are down 10 percent to 15 percent. You must bulletproof the HNW portfolio. The theme is to structure the portfolio for consistency. Sure, we gave up returns in 1998 and 1999—but look at what we did in 2000!

"What keeps me up at night? Ways to provide clients with an edge. Ways to provide value-added service. The markets and the tax laws are so complex that we must stay ahead of the curve in order to give the best possible advice."

What about professional designations? "Intrinsically, they mean a lot. If you understand the quantitative issues and can explain them in an understandable way, the certification becomes less important." Lori has the CIMA. "Staying away from the jargon is another key! Too many professionals use it."

The Web? "The upside of the Internet is that it gives you access to information. The downside is that it gives you access to information. Clients do no better by making decisions on their own. The problem is how the information is applied and used. The do-it-yourselfer has gone away as a result of 2000."

As far as prospecting is concerned, Lori does not do cold calling. Her business is almost all referral. She believes there is room for people who cold call, and she has one colleague who is outstanding at it. But Lori has earned a good reputation in certain communities, and that word of mouth leads to business generation. "Your name really can get around—it's the concept of six degrees of separation. If you do a great job, the results can be fantastic in certain circles. If you do a bad job, it can kill you."

The future? "Advisors who have built single platforms and do only one thing will go out of business. Clients want to turn to one person or one group or one place to get the highest level of advice and service. While they don't necessarily want one advisor, they want one person to lead the way. Product orientation is going out the window. It floors me that many folks actually look at the business this way."

KEEPING THE CLIENT ON BOARD
BY KEEPING THE CLIENT INFORMED

Steve B.
Former wirehouse advisor now with an independent broker-dealer
Englewood, Colorado

Steve met Steve B. when he was a retail broker at a major wirehouse, where he had been for 19 years. Today, he has $250 million to $300 million in assets and 500 clients. His average relationship is approximately $500,000 to $600,000. He is not interested in ultra-high-net-worth individuals; his ideal accounts are mom-and-pop clients who want to make sure they have enough to retire.

"We try to add more value to client relationships every day. We always ask them the question, Do you have enough to retire?" Steve uses what he calls a Retirement Sufficiency Analysis (RSA) when engaging a relationship. The process uses historical rates of return for stocks, bonds, and cash to determine whether the client's assets will be sufficient to live comfortably, given his or her goals.

A good example of Steve's approach can be illustrated by the experience of a recent new client. The client, in his early 50s, wants to retire in two years. He started in July 2000 with $2.5 million, and then proceeded to lose $250,000 in the market turmoil. The client naturally began to feel uneasy, so Steve performed an RSA and "stress tested" the account reflecting 10 percent and 20 percent declines to identify potential income flow. "We do these types of tests as needed to provide a high comfort level to our clients," says Steve.

"We are also unique in that every Monday we e-mail a market commentary to all of our clients who have e-mail. The commentary is usually 500 to 600 words long and keeps communication lines open by giving the client an opportunity to reply. It saves me a tremendous amount of time. I can look at the comments anytime and don't need to worry as much about phone calls.

"Our philosophy is to overdeliver and underpromise. Example: a client recently sold his business and had a lot of cash. He was very unhappy with his current advisor who was putting him into 'nickel stocks'—a classic way for a trader to earn commissions. The client was referred to me and said he loved our communiqués; he never heard from a broker as frequently as he had from us. I told the client, 'I am your CFO and I report to you!'"

Steve said there is a high demand for his level of service and he has no real fears about the business. "The real question is, 'How will we do a better job and what can we do to bring more value to the client?' Clients should be debt-free. We are in a storm right now and being debt-free is how you can weather it. If you have free cash flow it should be invested."

After the initial meeting with a client, Steve sends a letter of recommendation with a checklist that is used to monitor progress. This checklist identifies what the client's needs are.

"My ideal client is a delegator who trusts me, is an adult, is honest, will work with me, and has a long-term perspective. The ideal client is like a three-legged stool: he wants my advice; he follows my advice; and he pays for my advice."

TRADITIONAL VALUES + TECHNOLOGY = LOOK OUT!

Harry R. Tyler
President, Tyler Wealth Counselors, Inc.
West Chester, Pennsylvania

Founded in 1988 by Harry Tyler as Tyler Consulting, Inc. and purchased in 2000 by Commonwealth Bancorp., Inc. of Norristown, Penn., Tyler Wealth Counselors is a financial advisory firm focusing on high-net-worth individuals. Tyler, a Certified Financial Planner, Chartered Financial Consultant, and Chartered Life Underwriter, began his career in insurance and pension sales. He created his financial advisory business to enjoy a good income and favorable working environment but also to create significant value as an ongoing entity that could be transferable. Here's how he did it, using a combination of traditional values and high technology.

"You can see our approach on our Web site, <www.tylerwealth .com>. Our message is 'We bring your money to life.' After decades of helping people achieve financial success, we have learned that money's greatest value is not determined merely by numbers on statements or in portfolios. Rather, money's most lasting value comes from the freedom it gives people—and the plans they are able to make—when they no longer have to worry about their own financial security. We go beyond conventional planning and want clients to be excited about what their money is doing today and what it will do in the future. We ask them to tell us what's most important to them, and what they would most like to accomplish with their money and their lives.

"On our Web site, we list the chief concerns of our clients and ask whether the prospect shares these questions:

- Can I retire early?
- What choices should I make about my pension—lump-sum or monthly payments?
- What about my company stock or stock options?
- What are the tax consequences?
- What if my pension is inadequate?
- What about my postretirement insurance needs?
- Am I paying more taxes than necessary?
- How long will my money last?
- Can I generate more income and still get more growth?
- What about estate planning?
- How can I invest with lower risk and higher return?
- How much can I give away to my children without risking my own financial security?
- What about long-term care?
- Is my spouse prepared to be alone?
- What issues should we consider when making our plan?
- What can I do now to ensure my spouse's financial security?
- Who should my spouse rely on for advice on financial matters when I'm gone?
- Do I have more assets than I need?
- How much can I give away now and still have enough money for my lifetime?
- Can I help others without risking my own financial security?
- What kind of legacy would I like to leave?
- What's the best way to help a charity?
- Should I donate stocks or cash?

- Can I give away ownership of assets without giving up income?
- Are there tax benefits to charitable giving during my lifetime?
- How do I want to be remembered?
- Am I too busy to look after my own financial security?
- How can I maximize the benefits from stock options, pension, and benefit plans?
- Is my investment portfolio sufficiently diversified?

"Finally, for business owners, we pose:

- How can I maximize my business ownership without putting my financial security at risk?
- Is too much of my personal net worth tied to the business?
- What about retirement?
- What if I get sick?
- When's the right time to sell the business?
- Who will run the business when I retire or die?
- How does my business planning affect my retirement security and estate planning?

"We update our Web material with what we believe are interesting and nontechnical items on taxes, estate planning, and insurance. We did a fun and effective item that we called 'Top Ten Reasons Not to Buy Long-Term Care Insurance.' We said: 'In the format made famous by a favorite late-night-show host, we have compiled the ten best excuses ever heard for not buying a quality LTC plan:

10. Medicare will take care of me.
9. I will give my assets to my children and Medicaid will pay the bills.
8. My daughter-in-law is a nurse and will care for me.
7. The government will solve this problem before I need LTC.
6. I expect to stay healthy and will never need care.
5. If I never need insurance, I have wasted money.
4. I can always do it later.

3. It costs too much for adequate coverage.

2. Our investment net worth exceeds $1 million. We will self-insure.

1. I don't know a good advisor who can tell me if I really need coverage.'"

FOCUS: MANAGED ACCOUNTS

Scott W.
President, independent advisory firm
Dallas, Texas

"We are an affiliate of a large independent broker-dealer and have five people on staff: my partner, an analyst, an operations manager, a support person, and myself. We have $200 million in assets under management, representing 170 households. Virtually all our business is done in separately managed accounts. Our minimum account size is $1 million, although we take a few smaller accounts that have growth potential, and our typical client has $750,000 to $2 million in liquid assets. Most of our clients are business owners and professionals, and most are in their early 50s. We don't get into estate planning or insurance, which we refer to others when appropriate.

"When the market turned down in 2000, we made a strategic point of having a face-to-face meeting with every client in the fourth quarter. Not every client took us up on our offer, but most did. The purpose of the meeting was to provide comfort and eliminate panic calls. Actually, on a relative basis, our strategic discipline in asset allocation resulted in good performance. One client insisted that we give $100,000 of his assets to a manager who was 'hot.' We resisted, wrestled with him, and ultimately convinced him not to do it. It turned out that the manager was down significantly for the quarter.

"Another story relates to a personal friend who came to us for advice. His broker, also an acquaintance of ours, had invested 70 percent of his $500,000 portfolio in tech stocks, and more than half of that was invested in just nine companies. We explained that his portfolio was too concentrated, and that his problem was that he was exposed to significant downside risk. While we urged him to diversify immediately, he didn't want to pay our fees or sell securities and incur a tax bill. He told us he'd do fine. Needless to say, his portfolio tanked and he lost several hundred thousand dollars. Had he taken our suggestion, he probably would have paid us $5,000, which was minimal considering his actual loss.

"I have a CIMA designation, but I think the CFP is the one that really matters. It's the one that the general public understands, and it has the highest recognition. The designations are of most importance to younger advisors who are trying to build credibility."

DR. QUARTERBACK

Gerry D.
Senior vice president, wirehouse
Hartford, Connecticut

"After 17 years on the institutional side of the business, I decided at age 42 to move to the retail side in 1989. I had no assets and no income, but I took my professionalism from the institutional business, got myself computerized, and farmed out money management to others. Today, I have more than $700 million under management, and I did $2.23 million in 2000. My typical clients are married couples where the husband is a corporate executive. They're 40 to 55 years old and have assets between $500,000 and $30 million. I have 125 clients, all in managed accounts, and my top 35 clients represent 80 percent of my assets.

"The business has changed over the past five years. The phrase 'investment management consultant' was the catchphrase. Today, that's less important than life planning, protecting assets, and bequeathing assets. Curiously, long-term care is one key missing piece in most plans. Our approach is to help clients with their lives; investment management is part of that. A significant amount of money is coming to us from retirement plans, so wealth advice is turning into a big business.

"My approach is to go for all of the assets; we want to know where everything is and try not to be in a horse race to capture assets. We also track out-of-custody assets, but push the client to consolidate. It is important to be the quarterback. We try to get the client in front of our estate planning professionals whenever possible to help capture assets. We only focus on serious money, and if the individual wants a trading account he or she can go somewhere else because we don't want any 'funny money.' We view ourselves as the doctor, and writing a prescription without a diagnosis is malpractice. We don't say this stuff to be lofty or obnoxious, but we want to be held accountable and to do that we must know where the client's 'stuff' is. We encourage clients to stay away from the hot Internet stocks, telling them to think long term and recommending that they do nothing when nothing is the right thing to do. We send clients letters, notes, and thoughts about the market when appropriate.

"One of our biggest concerns is staying ahead of the curve. The business is evolving very rapidly and you need to understand as much about product development as possible. It's a tough time to get started for a new broker. Wall Street needs to partner trainees with guys who have been in the business for a while. They need to extend the after-training payout by moving it from 12 to 18 months, as some firms have done. You have to give the new consultant time to build relationships, given the competitive nature of this business. It's frustrating not having enough time to get the business where it needs to be and not being able to do more 'warm and fuzzy' work with clients."

BUILDING SCALE TO HELP CLIENTS

Ron Weiner, CFP
President, Retirement Design & Management, Inc.
Westport, Connecticut

"I've been involved in the planning industry for a long time. I've been a member of the International Association of Financial Planners since 1976. I began my own practice in 1986, and before that I was in wholesaling and management at a broker-dealer.

"I went back into management, helping to create the financial planning department at Oppenheimer and serving as the senior vice president of the Retirement Group at Cowen and Co. In 1990, I created Retirement Design & Management, Inc. (RD&M). We grew very fast because of what I believe to be the most efficient service model for building a firm. RD&M currently has approximately $350 million in assets under management, representing approximately 180 families. Our typical client has well over $1 million in assets with us. Clients are typically older individuals, either successful businesspeople or retirees. Many, in fact, are CPAs and attorneys. Our clients typically do not use the Internet very much, though about 20 percent of them would like strictly electronic statements. We have approximately $250 million in discretionary management accounts (approximately 400), which are about half stocks and half funds. Accounts under $100,000 we place in mutual fund asset allocation programs. We do not use wrap fee managers, except when large clients would like diversification from our management style. In that case, they either find their own money managers or we select money managers for them.

"RD&M has a staff of 14 people, all on salary. Bonuses are paid, like on Wall Street, at the end of the year, depending on the performance of their sectors and the firm as a whole. We have five MBAs, one master's in economics, and numerous other designations within the firm. We even have a certified divorce planner on the board.

"One of the keys to our success is working closely throughout the year with clients' attorneys and accountants. We may have to speak to clients' other professionals two or three times a month to resolve planning or strategic issues. We found that our clients and their professional counselors often do not talk to each other. We force them to do that. When we ask a wealthy client about a financial screwup in their lives, we can usually trace the problem back to a lack of communication among that client's different counselors.

"Another effort we make to stay close to clients is to send them frequent newsletters. Last year amid all the market turmoil we increased communications. We gained 30 new clients and lost just one. The one we lost was costing us too much in time and effort, anyway.

"In my opinion, the biggest problem with the advice business today involves scale. Our business requires knowledge in sales, trusts, taxes, and operations. It is very difficult for one person or a two- to three-person shop to have excellent command of all the different skills. The larger the scale, the more experts you need to have in-house and the better you can serve clients. By being both detailed financial planners and discretionary money managers, we are afforded significant insights into the needs of our clients and are able to act with speed when allocating or reallocating portfolios. Obviously, the greater the scale, the greater the value of the firm."

LEVERAGING INSIGHT AND UNDERSTANDING

Elizabeth W.
Team banker with international clients
Miami, Florida

Elizabeth began her career in 1980 while studying international banking and finance. She had some contact with HNW clients at that time. She moved into banking operations and finally private banking. She traveled to Venezuela and the Caribbean to work with offshore HNW clients and became a junior banking officer. Her big advantage was understanding operations, which enhanced her client relations. In 1992, Elizabeth joined a major wirehouse as an overseas financial consultant.

"My team has $500 million in assets under management and about 200 client relationships. Our typical client is a family man in his late 50s who's very involved in business. He has a net worth of about $15 million and liquid wealth of about $8 million to $10 million. My clients don't call me every day or every week. They trust me, and we meet once a quarter. I also have close relationships with their wives, who frequently have a tremendous influence on investment decisions. Compared to other professionals, I believe I have a unique advantage being a woman. I am able to develop very warm and genuine relationships with my clients.

"Right now we're focusing heavily on estate planning and estate taxes. We're also looking to use insurance to protect clients whose beneficiaries are U.S. residents."

What's scary right now and keeps her awake? The declining stock market worries her, particularly since many of her clients are so heavily influenced by TV and other media. Her clients were never exposed to so much financial news, but now everyone watches CNBC, receives business journals, and listens to Bloomberg. This trading mentality is creating significant short-term problems. During 2000, Elizabeth took her clients by the hand and said they sometimes got tired of what she had to say about not focusing on the short term. Fortunately, none of her clients thinks the world is ending; her clients understand that the market has to correct itself and does go through cycles. She is explaining that we are basically in a "blip."

What about technology? "Many of my clients are now using the Internet for investment information purposes. Some of them are doing their own trading. But thanks to the year 2000, that trend is dying. Many of the clients are back to where they started after being enamored with an endlessly rising market. The HNW client is not customarily familiar with a margin call. Can you imagine what that feels like to someone who does not understand what's going on? Fortunately, much of this is being experienced by the younger generation and not the older client."

MEETING ESTATE NEEDS WITH FIRM SUPPORT

Allan E.
Senior wirehouse advisor
Chicago, Illinois

"Most of my clients are in their early 60s and most are business owners or prominent doctors and attorneys.

"As a wealth manager, I approach my clients with a formalized policy statement. It shows that I am process-driven rather than product-driven. I focus on the corpus of the principal and keeping it intact. I view my job as understanding absolute rates of return, understanding the client's lifestyle needs, and how that relates to the client's capital. This mandates an approach that's different from my peers. First, my clients and I agree on a specified rate of return, and then I seek a judicious balance of risk and return after I understand their risk tolerance."

Allan's biggest concern is the lengthy retirement of many affluent clients. "Average retirement occurs at approximately age 63. The average life of a Caucasian male at age 63 is 84.6 years. A post-retirement need of 21 years is both apparent and frightening. Most people haven't made the plan for 21 years of life expectancy. Since many clients will outlive the corpus of their principal, they must be educated to understand that asset allocation must be more aggressive than originally thought. Many clients claim they can't weather variability, and want to put their assets in fixed-income securities. The reality is that you need a more aggressive mix, and the challenge is in helping the client handle this approach. The life expectancy for females—90—presents even more of a challenge."

What does Allan say to today's HNW practitioners? "Become a specialist; develop an expertise in understanding the HNW market. Years ago, we were more product generalists. Today we need to become experts. Understand, in particular, today's hardware and software, and have superior quantitative skills. Begin with financial planning analysis and know it inside and out. Develop estate planning expertise and understand how to mitigate estate planning consequences. Learn about second-to-die insurance, and revocable and irrevocable trusts. And become expert in estate planning tools."

Because of the complexities of estate planning for affluent clients, Allan will bring a member of his firm's estate planning group into many meetings. "As a HNW advisor, you must try to show uniqueness and value-added service in the marketplace. Everyone purports to be a consultant. You must differentiate yourself from the herd at your first meeting or your chance of closing an account is severely diluted."

SMALL TOWN, BIG SUCCESS

Gary Rathbun
CEO, Private Wealth Consultants
Toledo, Ohio

"I began my career as a life insurance agent at New York Life in 1981. I slowly became involved in financial planning, and after a few years passed licensing tests to sell mutual funds and, later, general securities. I'm a Chartered Life Underwriter, a Chartered Financial Consultant, and hold a master's degree in financial services.

"Five years ago we decided to go entirely fee-based, although we still take commissions on life insurance sales. The five-person staff and I manage $100 million in assets for about 60 clients and charge a maximum of 100 basis points (bps), although most clients pay about 75 to 80 bps. For about 15 clients, I act as a personal chief financial officer.

"Most of these clients own their own businesses and are the proverbial millionaire next door. Their median age is about 60; their net worth from $5 million to $10 million (although I have two whose net worth is $20 million); and they usually have between $1 million and $5 million in investable assets. We plan 17 contacts a year with each client, which includes e-mails, phone calls, sending articles and cassettes, and in-person visits. I also send clients gifts of books from time to time on subjects that have nothing to do with finance or business, just because I know they'd like them.

"My specialty is charitable estate planning. I've written books on the subject (*The Charitable Giving Handbook,* National Underwriters; *The Perfect Legacy,* High Net Worth Press), and that has helped attract national clients.

"Before coming to our firm—typically for estate planning, to start—most of our affluent clients used the services of a major brokerage firm. They like what I can bring to the table.

"One business-owner client who bought insurance from me had a $5 million credit line with a major Cleveland-area bank. He mentioned that he wanted a $1.5 million loan from the bank to rebuild his truck distributorship after a case of embezzlement on the part of a former employee, but the bank was balking. I took on the role of personal CFO and went to another bank to negotiate. I got my client better terms on his line of credit, as well as a loan at a favorable rate of interest. For other clients, I've arranged car loans, found new accountants, and gathered information needed by accountants. Since I started to build a strategic network early on in my career, I got to know trust attorneys and private client guys at the local banks. Now, I can play the banks against each other to get my clients the best deals.

"I live my life by two questions: Who am I serving? and Am I doing what I'm doing for the money? If I am serving the client and doing the right thing for them, regardless of the money, I'm satisfied. I don't accept bank finder fees or other fees for steering business to particular institutions. I disclose all commissions and fees to customers and staff, so everyone knows how much we earn from any particular activity. We don't manage money directly; we use Nicholas-Applegate and Atalanta Sosnoff, and we keep up-to-date risk tolerance and investment policy statements for our clients. I'll even set up an E*Trade account for a client who wants to have fun. I tell them that speculating is not what a CFO does. So they keep track of what they do and it serves as their entertainment.

"When I switched from commissions to fees, it took two years to make up the lost income, but now that the transition is behind me, I feel as if I am overpaid. We add about 10 to 12 new clients a year and lose a few, largely as a result of death. My goal is to serve just 20 clients, with $5 million to $10 million in investable assets each."

If the stories of these advisors raise questions in your mind, perhaps you will find some answers in the following chapter.

Chapter *8*

*B*ecoming a Wealth Manager

Five steps you can take to get there.

Do you want to become a wealth manager? Are you getting there? The Gresham Company, LLC has developed a five-step process to becoming a wealth manager. Following these basic steps can help you start the transition from a transactional financial advisor to a fee-based wealth manager. Measure yourself using these tools and find out.

STEP 1: IDENTIFY YOUR TARGET MARKET

The best way to begin building your wealth-management prospect list is by looking at the market you know best: your own clients. Screen your existing client base and make a list of all those with high net worth. Refine the list by searching for clients who meet one or more of the following criteria:

- They add assets to their accounts.
- They refer clients to you.
- They purchase several products or services per account.
- They generally follow your advice.

STEP 2: ENGAGE THE CLIENT

Your goals are to schedule face-to-face meetings with clients to explain the meaning of wealth management, as well as to overcome their perception of you as an undifferentiated broker/salesperson/ investment specialist. Currently, they probably think of your role narrowly; they may be uncertain how a change in that role affects them.

The most logical approach to initiating such a meeting is probably to ask for a client review session. You might say something like this:

> *We haven't talked in person recently about the things we're doing for you. Let's get together next week to review your situation.*

You might also position the request as an opportunity to talk about the client's goals for the future, or about a particular concern. You know the client best, so use the approach that is most appropriate in each instance.

In preparation for the meeting, prepare an agenda that will review:

- **Client expectations.** This will build on the concerns and issues you've talked about in previous meetings.
- **Current product and service offerings.** Be up-to-date on all investments you've sold them, the status of these investments, and the outlook for the future.
- **Potential questions or complaints.**

Preparation is very important in order to start positioning yourself as a wealth manager. You don't want to waste time and momentum by focusing on past performance or by becoming defensive about a particular investment suggestion.

Before the meeting, also check the age of every member of the client's household and immediate family, if that information is available. The idea is not to go into the meeting prepared to tell the client what their needs are (or to sell them a product based on your perceptions), but to familiarize yourself with logical areas you'll want to probe for issues and concerns. If you know the client has a ten-year-old child, for example, you'll want to discuss college savings. If you know the client's goal is to retire early, you'll want to ask if he or she is thinking about meeting the financial demands of caring for aging parents.

STEP 3: IDENTIFY THE UNMET NEED

As discussed in Chapter 4, client financial and life needs fall into five general categories: estate planning, retirement planning, income protection, assisting children, and assisting parents. We call this The Big Picture. When you demonstrate an awareness of and concern for these major overall needs—in a new and more comprehensive way that goes beyond your traditional approach—you establish and reinforce your position as a wealth manager. Increasing the client's comfort and confidence in your ability to manage his or her wealth, not just his or her investments, is a key goal of your initial client meeting.

Here are some things you can say to ease into these discussions:

> As I review your relationship, I see we've talked a lot about investing for retirement. What we haven't talked much about is the emotional and financial impact of having to care for your parents, which could affect your retirement. How do you feel about that?

> As a financial advisor, there are many things I worry about on behalf of my clients. I know you have many financial con-

cerns, and I want to make sure we're handling them. So, as I think about helping you manage your wealth, I wonder if you've taken care of _____.

Looking at the various pieces of The Big Picture—and asking questions about wills, beneficiaries, long-term care, disability insurance, and the many other issues that fall under these headings—doesn't mean you have to address every problem all at once. It's best to discuss just two or three important needs at each meeting. The Big Picture provides a framework for identifying, categorizing, and methodically solving a client's needs, but you don't want to overwhelm the client or yourself. Leave the door open for future discussions, and over time you can address all the client's wealth-management issues.

Another helpful tool is to fill in the Future Shock table with a client. (See Figure 8.1.) This exercise should help lead clients to three major insights:

1. It's later than they think in terms of plotting a wealth-management strategy.

FIGURE 8.1

Sample Future Shock Grid

Ages	Now	2005	2010	2015	2020	2025	2030
Spouse							
Spouse							
Child 1							
Child 2							
Parent(s)							

2. Their needs are more complex than they realize.

3. They need to do something now.

Here's why the Future Shock exercise works: The best advisors bond with their clients around a shared vision of the client's future. Since the client's view of the future forms the basis for the advisor's work, the key question advisors must ask clients—as clearly as possible—is: "If you could look into a crystal ball and see the future, what would it look like for you and your family?"

The success of many top advisors results from their ability to help clients see the future and to make the key financial decisions to realize their goals. Getting clients to share their hopes and fears about the future can cement enduring client relationships. But many advisors are hesitant to probe, fearing they will scare off clients by prying into their private thoughts. And many clients indeed are reluctant to share their dreams. They're not used to trusting financial advisors with these intimate thoughts. But since honest information is necessary to develop a productive relationship, this communication gap must be closed. How to do that?

Determining Dreams

The answer comes not from a major brokerage firm or university or consulting firm. Rather, it comes from the pulpit of a small-town church. It was there that an extraordinary minister offered his method of helping others see the future. And although he didn't intend his process for financial advisors, it is probably the most effective method of promoting meaningful advisor-client dialogue on the subject of the future.

The minister was a great communicator. Parishioners of all ages were drawn to him for both his compassion and his candor. Like most good advisors, he was a good listener. Also like great advisors, he could challenge the opinions of his "clients" and probe for more information. His personality allowed him a range of communication beyond that of ordinary counselors.

One group concerned the minister: young couples. He had seen the growth of divorce and watched too many young people leave home to get married at too young an age. Typically driven by the romance of life beyond their small town—or just romance—the kids wanted out. They would stop by the minister to say good-bye or as a way to mollify a desperate parent. He tried different arguments, but felt his entreaties were falling on deaf ears. The kids usually were polite, but their resolve was steeled prior to the meeting. He usually couldn't talk them out of their plans, and couldn't get them to consider the impact on their future from their actions today. He needed something to shock his clients. He needed a way to show them the future today.

One day, he told a young couple, "Let's look into the future; let me take you on a fantasy trip." He took out a plain piece of paper and wrote down their names. Next to each name he wrote their ages. Above the ages, he wrote the year.

"Here's where you are today," he reported. "You're ready to take on the world. I envy you. Let me help you plan for the future."

Importantly, he didn't challenge their plans. He didn't lecture. He returned to his paper and began listing the parents and other people he knew to be important to the couple. He asked them for other names when he exhausted his memory. Ages were listed next to each name, even if it meant guessing a little. He asked about children (in some cases, the couple was already expecting) and began to work up a chart with all the names and ages in their places. (See Figure 8.2.)

The minister now had a framework in which to discuss the couple's plans. He could refer to a year in the future and ask what they thought might be happening at that time. "So, you plan to have family right away? Do you think that may impact earning enough for a house?" or "You both plan to work for a few years, buy a house, and then start a family. When do you think that will be?" The chart allowed the couple to consider their future based on an objective framework of dates and ages. He didn't have to editorialize because the facts were right in front of them. The minister used

FIGURE 8.2

Future Shock Grid and the Minister

Ages	Now	2005	2010	2015	2020	2025	2030
Spouse	37	41	46	51	56	61	66
Spouse	37	41	46	51	56	61	66
Child 1	4	8	13	18	23	28	33
Child 2		4	9	14	19	24	29
Mom	62	66	71	76	81	86	91

the facts in the form of ages and dates to stimulate conversation with the "clients" about what the future held in store.

While planning for kids and homes were the most common near-term issues raised in the fantasy trip, other important topics came up. If the couple planned to have children, did the mother plan to work after the births or stay home? Would the earnings of one parent be enough to support the family? Had the couple considered the impact of lost wages? What about retirement? Sure, retirement seems like a lifetime away to a young couple, and it is, but a little planning can help avoid some of the strain that is all too evident among older relatives who have not taken the steps needed to provide for retirement. Does your employer offer a pension plan? Do you save? How much do you think you'll need?

Another tough issue for any family is the care of older relatives. Because the fantasy trip contrasts the age of family members at different times in the future, it becomes easier to see potential lifestyle conflicts. For example, a couple may be able to meet the financial demands of raising children, but be unprepared to care for a parent who suffers a medical setback. A 1997 study of more than

1,500 people found that one out of every four families had at least one member who provided care for an elderly relative or friend in the previous year. The costs of being a caregiver go beyond the out-of-pocket expenses of food and shelter. Medical services, pharmaceuticals, and transportation can be more significant, and less predictable. Reviewing the fantasy trip age chart with clients can be the first step to prepare more knowledgeably for the needs of older relatives. Parents living comfortably on their own at age 65 may suffer medical setbacks requiring your clients to provide support. When are your clients at risk for being caregivers? Our small-town minister was able to get many of his young couples to see that their parents would need help just at the time the couple's kids would be leaving home. The fantasy trip does its job by projecting a view of the future—a view based entirely on the reality of age.

Apply the fantasy trip to your clients. Get clients to consider not just the implications of their goals—such as saving for kids' college or their retirement—but also for the lifestyle implications of aging parents, second marriages, and kids returning to live at home after college. Financial plans typically focus on personal financial needs. They seldom consider the unexpected demands of other people. Since one of four families provides some kind of elder care, are your clients ready for that role? In many communities, more than one-quarter of the families have a child living at home who is over the age of 21. Have your clients assessed the potential of sharing their retirement with an adult child nearby? We know that many clients worry about these issues, but just as many have avoided planning for their potential cost. The fantasy trip helps draw out the concerns so you can help develop the solutions.

STEP 4: CREATE A BLUEPRINT FOR ACTION

After you've given your client a clear view of the future and brought overlooked financial needs to their attention, it's time to provide solutions. Your action plan requires three elements:

1. **A clear need.** Select one of the important needs identified in your initial meeting and gain the client's agreement to address it.
2. **A way to translate the need into investment language.** If you use managed accounts, you and your client can fill out its investment questionnaire. The form identifies the client's investment objective, time horizon, risk tolerance, and performance expectations, and serves as the basis for producing an actionable plan.
3. **An actionable plan to address the financial need.** The client's completed managed account program questionnaire will generate an investment policy statement, which outlines the funding mechanism to meet the client's need. You will have, at the end, a portfolio of funds or separately managed accounts from which the client may choose.

STEP 5: DEVELOP A PLAN FOR AN ONGOING CLIENT RELATIONSHIP

Regularly scheduled client meetings are critical to establishing and maintaining your position as the client's primary source of financial information. Schedule quarterly meetings with a specific agenda to provide feedback and fresh input. The agenda should include the following:

- **A review of old business.** Review the last meetings, as well as the advisor and client to-do lists.
- **Review results.** Look at account statements, managed account reports, and performance versus goals.
- **Discuss new business.** Probe for concerns using The Big Picture chart (see Figure 4.1), identify needs, and develop action steps.
- **Schedule next meeting.**

Chapter **9**

Measure Your Success

Use these three success metrics as a self-assessment.

Should you change your business model? If you're not doing as well as you would like, it may be time to consider a change. Or perhaps you're doing well on several levels, but, like many successful advisors, you feel a nagging sense of self-doubt. What Intel CEO Andy Grove once called the "paranoia" needed for business success can rob you of the enjoyment you owe yourself and your family.

Before you change your business, take time to assess yourself as an advisor. The process will provide the calm necessary to enjoy life and to help plan your future. Much like a medical checkup or a report card, a good way to assess your business self is by using a grading system to measure how you're doing relative to your goals and expectations.

Here's a grading system that uses three measures of success.

SUCCESS METRIC #1: ADDITIONAL ASSETS

Successful financial advisors run their practices like businesses. They meet client needs with a view to the future. Evidence of a good business model is found in the additional investments made by satisfied clients. When clients are happy with their advisors, these advisors—not others—get new investment money. Though some clients may make additional investments with you out of habit or inertia, affluent clients typically diversify their assets and give new cash flows to other advisors if they are not delighted with your services.

The metric of additional investment is an especially critical benchmark when working with the affluent, since most affluent clients are businesspeople. Most draw a modest income from their business during the year and then take a substantial profit-sharing cut when the year-end results are tallied and taxes determined. It is at this critical stage that the business owner decides where to send new profits. This is the time when your value as an advisor is re-vealed. If your client chooses to send you more money, this is con-firmation of the value of your relationship. Even if your client notifies you of the looming cash distribution and asks for your ad-vice, other providers may be in the mix also. A client may decide his or her account with you is "too big" and that having "too many eggs in one basket"—yours—warrants additional thought about where the money might go.

A random survey of million-dollar clients at one wirehouse in April 2000 (a time when the Nasdaq Index fell 349 points) revealed that 80 percent had accounts with online providers in addition to their full-service accounts at the wirehouse. In fact, the typical mil-lionaire client has three or four primary financial advisory rela-tionships. Where would new money from these clients go—online or to one of several full-service accounts?

Not receiving additional investments from a business owner every year is a warning sign. It may indicate a change in your relationship with that client. One possibility is that your client may be giving the annual profit-sharing distribution to another advisor. While you may not welcome the arrival of another advisor, you should accept that person if a service you don't offer is being provided. Complementary relationships are inevitable; they should be acknowledged by you and your client.

It's also possible that your client's business is not as profitable as it has been in the past. This is critical information. Business owners typically derive a huge share of their self-esteem from the success of their business. If deteriorating business conditions put pressure on the owner, the decline can be traumatic. Your role as an advisor includes the need to support your best clients when they need your help. While a client may be protective of the information that the business is not doing well, he or she is more likely to welcome the opportunity to share the burden with a trusted advisor.

To measure the inflow of additional assets, use this checklist to develop a worksheet. You can use it as a tickler, reminding you to talk to your self-employed clients about the state of their business and about potential additional investments.

Additional Asset Checklist

- List your top 20 clients.

- List the number of clients that added additional money in the past 12 months.

- Specify the amount of money added by each client.

- List the date(s) when additional investments were made. Go back to previous years, if possible, and note the dates. This may reveal when the client takes a business distribution.

- If you are not sure of the distribution date, ask the client and note the date.

- Note the date of the business's fiscal year-end.

SUCCESS METRIC #2: REFERRAL BUSINESS

Referral business is another critical success measurement of a financial advisory practice. Many affluent clients are seeking a high-quality advisor, and our studies of top advisors indicate they receive most of their new business from client referrals. Faced with the need to identify good financial advisors, most affluent clients trust each other more than any other source. In fact, clients may unwittingly give referrals, as evidenced by the rising tide of "implied" referrals. These are the cases in which a prospect appears at your door because you work with a friend or colleague—even though the friend (and your client) hasn't made a formal referral and isn't even aware the prospect is seeking your counsel. The old training approach of asking clients for referrals is slipping away. Service-hungry affluent clients typically do not want their valued financial advisor to serve many other similar clients. How many clients do you think your affluent clients want you to have? We'll bet the most common answer is "one"—just them. But if your clients are satisfied with your service and understand your need to replenish your client list or slightly expand it, they probably will be willing to help.

Referral Business Checklist

- List your top 20 clients.

- Note how you acquired each client.

- Note how many have provided referrals in the past year.

- Ask each top-20 client to step into your place and suggest what should be done to find more clients like him or her.

SUCCESS METRIC #3: NEW BUSINESS

In addition to additional investments from affluent clients and the flow of referral business, the third key indicator of a successful practice is the development of unrelated new business. This metric is of less concern if your practice is established and can claim good results against the first two benchmarks. Most top advisors claim not to market at all, noting that the bulk of their new clients come through referrals.

But the new practice must position itself to attract new clients without the benefit of a large client base providing new cash inflows and referrals. A true sales and marketing strategy is critical to the development of a young practice, and separate metrics determine the strategy's effectiveness and highlight areas in which improvements are needed. Because the procurement of affluent clients may take months or even years, a sales and marketing strategy cannot be evaluated on the basis of new clients and new assets alone. Metrics for the affluent investor market include the ability to get appointments with potential clients, indicating the relevance of a topic or approach to the marketplace that will eventually translate into new business. Constantly seek issues that worry your clients and find ways to reveal those concerns in your prospects.

An excellent example of a "concerns-based" affluent market sales campaign can be found in a highly successful insurance and benefits practice run by Steve W. in North Carolina. Many years ago Steve realized that affluent clients often worry about health care costs and the potential financial impact such costs could have on their retirement. At the same time, Steve and his agents faced increasing competition in attracting new clients using traditional insurance and investment products to solve the all-too-common needs of death insurance and retirement savings. Competing against an army of life insurance and mutual fund salespeople, Steve uses the long-term care story as an alternative marketing strategy to get the attention of affluent clients.

He and his colleagues contact individuals and discuss the potential risks and costs of long-term care. While most of the calls fail to result in appointments, every 300 calls yield an average of five prospects. These five prospects agree to a meeting with an agent and a sales manager. The agents seek information about the prospect's financial concerns and resources; the team assesses the needs and then explains the features and benefits of long-term care insurance. On average, three out of five appointments result in a sale, with the typical client having a net worth of about $1.5 million.

Once long-term care insurance is sold and their expertise as problem solvers established, agents often are able to leverage their entrée into additional product sales. The next service offered? Many times, it is a separately managed account—the assets for which are drawn from a smattering of mutual fund holdings and individual securities.

"Our clients revealed considerable financial data in the process of qualifying for their long-term care policy, so they feel more at ease with us as advisors," Steve says. "It's a good base from which to extend the relationship. The managed account is similar to a long-term care policy in its ability to relieve stress; the clients feel as though they have solved a problem, not just bought an investment."

Positioning the sale of a separately managed account *after* the sale of a long-term care policy is a better marketing approach than trying to sell a complex product after starting with, say, a mutual fund. A consultative, less-transactional sales style lends itself to selling more complex products over a longer period of time.

New Business Checklist

- List the number of appointments you set up each month with potential clients.

- List the chief products or services you use to prospect.

- If you use seminars to teach the basics of the area in which you specialize (long-term health care, for example, or estate planning, financial planning, investment advice, or business succession planning), record the number of attendees and those with whom you meet afterwards.

- If you do cold calling to set up in-person appointments, record the number of calls made, the number of appointments established, and the number of sales that result. Through this process, you will be developing a standard by which you can judge your future efforts.

- Similarly, if you do direct-response advertising—direct-mail pieces or invitations to a seminar, for instance—record the total number of pieces sent and the responses. Use these metrics to test your offer and copy.

Chapter *10*

*Y*our Questions Answered

Here are the questions advisors like you are asking.

In speaking with advisors across the country, Steve and Evan have the opportunity to find out what's on their minds. Advisors everywhere are concerned about competition, about gathering assets, and about meeting and exceeding the service expectations of their clients. The following are some of the specific questions the authors have been asked recently and their responses.

Who is likely to be the biggest competitive threat over the next five years?

Don't worry about traditional advisors more than you do currently. Sure, another advisor—whether from a securities firm, a bank, or an insurance company—may out-service you, but you've always handled that kind of competition. At the same time, don't worry about technology replacing you, either. Affluent investors won't give up dealing with a person no matter how advanced the technology becomes.

The real threat is some new kind of human-technical combination that will provide a much higher level of service than either humans or technology do now. Somebody is going to come up with a seamless technology to deliver essential banking and mortgage services and provide access to all other financial services. Put a caring human into that mix to effectively provide the service to the public and the game is over.

Doubt the potential? Look at other industries that are competing with Internet firms. By itself, no automobile dealer will be put out of business by the Web, but consider the impact created by the combination of Web sites like CarsDirect.com or autobytel.com. Armed with data about models and costs, a car buyer is much more informed, and enters the showroom with more confidence. The Web can provide information, but it can't replace the physical driving experience. The downside is that information clarity makes it harder for the dealer to maintain profit margins. The upside is that the sites probably help sell more cars because the buyers feel more confident. The key for service and product providers in all industries is to harness the power of the Web and other technology to better serve existing clients. Technology should be implemented in a way that frees and empowers humans to provide the personal service and individual attention that only a caring person can provide.

We've watched with fascination how a local bookstore in Madison, Conn.—R.J. Julia's, run by Roxanne Coady—has flourished in the era of Amazon and Barnes and Noble. Roxanne and her team have constantly monitored local preferences and adjusted accordingly, while employing the Web for information flow and technology to better track popular tastes. They actually know what their customers want to read and they find it. Sure, you can get a profile of your preferences on Amazon, but will Amazon tell you why *you* will like the book?

Who will be the supercompetitors and what should I do about them?

Big accounting firms have as good a chance as any to fill the space. Private banks are other candidates. And you can't count out big brokerage firms, which are starting to experiment with Schwab-like direct access to salaried representatives in high-tech call centers. When they start to see better margins from these direct clients than they do from advisor-served clients, watch for big changes.

Seemingly sudden changes based on new technology already have changed other industries. In a certain sense, that is the Wal-Mart story. The Arkansas-based retailer was able to grow from a core of small-town stores—which were not much different from the outlets of other retailers—because it employed inventory technology much more effectively than its competitors. In financial services, a firm that uses technology effectively could create a much more savvy and effective advisor.

*T*oday, most advisors underutilize technology and don't think of it as a strategic tool in their practices.

The challenge to independent reps will be that the larger firms have the capital to make the extraordinary investment all this technology will require. And it will be expensive. In the future, every service offering will be defined by three issues.

Open architecture. Clients will demand access to every product from their advisor. If a wirehouse can't or won't sell a Vanguard fund, to use just one example, clients will take their business elsewhere. If there's a product or service a client hears about on TV or reads about on the Internet or in a magazine, he or she will want access to that product. Today, clients may think it's peculiar that such an open marketplace doesn't quite exist. In the near future, they won't stand for it.

Aggregation. Clients already wonder, "Why does it take five statements to show me everything I own?" In the future, they won't tolerate this. They'll want everything about their personal wealth in one place—whether you or someone else (and that someone could be an Internet service) provides it. In a sense, they want their wealth management to be as convenient as their credit card management; they receive one Visa or MasterCard statement, not 20 different statements from gas stations, department stores, and restaurants.

Convenience. Clients will want their financial dealings to be convenient. Of course, the challenge is to interpret what they mean by convenience, which is extremely subjective. To some clients, convenience will mean having everything online so they can look at their wealth and their activity on their own time, at their convenience. To others, convenience will mean being able to talk to a real person at any time of the day or night and get the same information.

At some point in the future, every product will be available everywhere at some price. We'll be back to the level playing field—at least insofar as pricing is concerned—that existed in the regulated days. Only it will be even more competitive. Other providers will have access to as much information about your client as you do. At that point, the advisor will be forced to compete on the basis of service quality—because there will be no other differentiation.

What should I do now?

Advisors must start to make a major investment—up to about 10 percent of your gross revenue—in technology. You probably will need to replace many of your processes and procedures and automate virtually everything. You should probably consider hiring a technology consultant if you are an independent. If you are with a big firm, more of the technological tools are given to you, but that doesn't take you personally off the hook. You must learn all about the technology your firm provides and fill in the gaps with software from outside. Regardless of the source of your technology, you must be certain you have the right tools to fit your work and client profile.

In addition to an investment in the technology itself, you will need to make an investment of time to learn about your new tools. In fact, you should be spending as much time studying software as you do studying the stock market. Look at Web sites, read trade and computer magazines, and talk to other advisors around the country to find out what they're doing. Meetings of the major professional and trade groups—the Financial Planning Association, the Securities Industry Association, the Institute for Certified Investment Management, and the Investment Management Consultants Association—are great places to learn and share information about technology. Wholesalers and product companies have loads of material on their Web sites. Make accessing these sites a regular part of your day. Ultimately, technology will enable you to stand on your own.

How do I handle market downturns with clients who have never experienced one?

Many clients have never seen a down market. Even if they have, this may be the first one they've experienced where they have real money at stake.

During previous market downturns, when most advisors were transactional, the most common reaction was to run away and wait. Maybe you sold municipal bonds until the equity markets turned around. Now, with more advisors selling managed accounts, the portfolio managers are making the buy and sell decisions and a decline in portfolio values is a result of their actions, not yours. At the same time, you're the person who guided the selection of the manager and the person with whom the client is in contact. In short, you're the one who has to do the explaining.

At times of a market downturn, many clients complain they could have done as poorly as their managers did. The truth is that they probably would have done worse, and that's part of the message you should be telling them. Clients hire you to act when their emotions stand in the way of doing the right things themselves. When the market is down, the client's reaction probably is to sell. But you know that's precisely the wrong thing to do. Here are some explanations good advisors give to their clients in times of market stress:

- "You hired me to protect you from the human emotions connected with investing your own money, and we're doing that."
- "Doing nothing now is the opposite side of taking profits when the market is high. Remember when we discussed selling some holdings last year?"
- "It looks like everything is down at the moment, but markets have a way of turning around."

When things are going well and clients follow your advice, it's easy to believe that advisors are overpaid. But when things get tough and advisors have to fight the human tendency to run from pain, that's the time that advisors are underpaid.

What are the downsides of separately managed accounts?

The major negative of managed accounts is the communications gap. Because of the recordkeeping and information cycle, it takes several weeks for a client to know how his or her investment has performed. In fact, one of the most serious failings of the industry is its inability to get information to investors on a timely basis.

In the absence of information, the client's anxiety level is bound to rise. Clients get nervous when they don't know what's going on. That's why the best advisors are constantly calling their clients and communicating with them even when they don't have the manager's formal statement.

When you sell separately managed accounts, you must preempt traditional forms of written communications and talk to clients frequently. You can't wait for a statement. Fortunately, a lot of information is available online. Go online and download account values so you can tell the client what's happening. If they can access the information, make sure you review it together. Use the resources of the money management firm to help you. Firms usually prepare hard copy material, which often is available on their Web sites, to explain market activity and losses in value.

What's the optimal number of clients?

While there is no one correct answer for every advisor, the leading private banking firms typically limit the number of client relationships any advisor can maintain to 25 to 35. Ask yourself why they selected that number of family/client relationships. The answer is that an advisor can't keep track of more effectively.

Decide for yourself. If you were a client and were presented with two identical advisors—each of whom earned $300,000 a year from his or her business, but who did business in different ways—which one would you choose? The advisor who had more than 750 individual accounts, or the advisor who had fewer than 150 accounts, which translates into about 30 to 50 family relationships? Are the clients of the second advisor wealthier than the clients of the first advisor, or does the second advisor have more of his or her clients' money because he or she devotes more time to them?

Since there are only so many hours in the day, there is only so much time an advisor can devote to each client. When you have more clients, therefore, you can do less for them because you have less time per client available. When you do less for clients, their perception is that you are limited in what you can do for them. In short, the fewer clients you have, the more likely you are to increase your assets under management.

Should I feel compelled to convert to fees?

The entire fee versus commission argument is riddled with misperceptions. In surveys and in actual practice, three-quarters of affluent clients typically say they prefer fees to commissions. But that's as far as most questioning usually goes. In truth, if you probe investors more deeply and go beyond an either-or question, you'll find that most investors want a flat fee, not a percentage fee. And if you probe even further, most say they would like a performance-based fee most of all. So, all the talk about fees putting advisor and client on the same side of the table is only partly true—clients only want to pay advisors when an advisor makes money for them.

Of course, at the present time, most performance-based fees would be illegal. But the change is coming, driven by technology and the relentless pressure on costs. In fact, what we're seeing with index funds, stock baskets, and exchange-traded funds is the de facto creation of performance-based fees. These products create a floor for costs; anything you do in the way of active management is a derivative of this base cost.

Ultimately, however, the fee versus commission question goes back to what precisely the client perceives he or she is buying from you. If clients are hiring you to beat the market, they feel justified in not paying you if you don't beat the market. So, if your business is based on performance and picking winning investments, you must put all your energy into beating the market.

By contrast, if your clients pay you to improve their wealth, there are lots of ways to prove your worth aside from beating the stock market. The money that you save them—through effective estate planning or tax strategies, for example—could be worth a lot more to a wealth-oriented client than picking stock market winners.

So before you decide whether you should switch from commissions to fees, ask yourself these questions:

- Do you make money for people or do you save them money?
- What have you been hired to do?

- Have you asked your clients what they hired you to do?
- Do you know why clients truly are paying you?
- Have you asked them what you could do that would delight them?

Today, commissions are virtually free. Tomorrow, virtually everything else will be free, too—except advice and personal service.

Should I set a minimum account size?

If you truly want to concentrate on affluent clients, you should. You and your practice are defined by your clients. If you have many small clients, particularly if you are in a community where your target market moves in the same circles, you will be thought of as a small-time advisor. Wealthy clients don't like to associate with an advisor who serves less affluent clients.

On the other hand, you may not be temperamentally suited to serve very affluent clients. You must feel comfortable, not awed, when dealing with them, and you must feel confident that your advice is worth taking. If that's not the case, wait until you are more comfortable to make your move.

Another reason not to set a minimum involves practical reality: You have to eat today. For younger advisors building a business, that makes setting a minimum difficult. The best approach might be for you to serve your smaller clients very well and turn them into your ambassadors. As your ambassadors do their work, you'll create more clients, who are always the greatest source of new business. Then, when your book is bigger, you can start the refining process.

One way to raise minimums gradually is to offer a multitier level of service—much as the airlines do with first, business, and coach classes of fares. This way, clients understand the level of service they will receive—meetings, updates, plans, etc.—before they receive it. At some level, every practice must set some objective limits, and this is one way to start.

What are the best products or services to emphasize?

The ones that have the greatest impact on the wealth of your client. Since most wealthy clients are business owners, think of the factors and forces that have the greatest impact on their wealth.

Naturally, their business is the biggest wealth-related part of their lives. What can you do to preserve the value of the business? Business value involves the ability to pass it on (which involves succession planning and business valuation), as well as estate taxes. You don't necessarily have to solve the problem, but are you facilitating the discussion? You have to become the point person. Obviously, no client relishes a discussion of estate planning, so most advisors simply avoid it. Don't! Insurance professionals have years of experience building safety nets—and now they are adding investments. If you are in the securities business, are you going to wait until all insurance agents sell investments before you decide to reciprocate the competition? Get over it, you're all in the same business.

Winning Tactic

Being a wealth manager involves building a safety net around a business owner.

How do I approach a business owner?

Since many business owners either have a natural sense of sales or have been approached by enough salespeople over time to understand sales psychology, there's not much you can do to "trick" a business owner into talking to you. Assume they know the ploy about calling their office at 7 AM to bypass the switchboard and their assistant. Assume they know every other tactic you might use to get them to answer the phone at work. And assume that they, like you, hate being called at home. So what do you do?

First, be true to your own style. Don't do anything that makes you feel uncomfortable. Next, gather information about the owner's business. That way, you'll feel confident when you ultimately speak. Next, write a very short (way less than one-page) handwritten note on nice stationery. The note should be hand-stamped and it should contain lots of white space. It should acknowledge that you understand the owner's business, and that you can offer a very specific benefit that you have provided to other business owners in similar situations. The benefit can be about lending, streamlining a retirement plan, cash management, or any other service your firm truly can perform well.

Unlike junk mail, a real first-class business communication is quite unusual. It will be read, and it will serve as evidence of your seriousness. The product or service should be something that saves a business owner time and/or money. Remember, making money is not the business owner's primary concern. If you can show a way to save money and time, the owner will listen and may become a client.

What's a reasonable income?

Let's work backwards. Suppose you can keep track of 30 families with assets that average $1.5 million each. That's $45 million in assets under management. Assuming a 1 percent gross, that's equal to $450,000 in gross revenue. Assuming a net of 35 percent to 50 percent, or slightly more, after expenses, if you are an independent advisor, that would mean an annual income of from $157,500 to more than $225,000, which exceeds the compensation of the average physician. That assumes 30 families to monitor, which compares to the 150 families most advisors serve. According to the Securities Industry Association, the average registered representative made about $175,000 in 1999. The Financial Planning Association says that the average independent financial planner earns between $79,000 and $120,000 a year, depending on his or her mix of business.

Is a professional designation worth the time and effort?

In a word, yes. Competition is intense; professional designations give an advisor an edge by diverting emphasis away from performance and toward useful knowledge.

Affluent clients often are forced to rely on performance when judging an advisor because there is no other objective standard to use. There is no advisor equivalent of a Michelin or Mobil Guide. Look at the explosion of interest that came out of nowhere when Morningstar introduced its star rankings to mutual funds. Some type of rating system like that is bound to come along for advisors. But until it does, clients are forced into making their own decisions about an advisor's competence. Referrals, of course, are an inferred indication of competence. You can improve your odds of receiving referrals and being selected by prospects by showing the commitment to your profession that a designation symbolizes.

In order to make a designation work for you, it must become central to your marketing efforts and not just letters after your name. You need to use your expertise constantly for the benefit of your clients and make them aware of it.

Appendix

| *A Directory of Designations*

Credentialism is alive and well in wealth management. Wealth advisors have found that the education and prestige conferred by having the appropriate designation can instill confidence in clients and prospects, and enhance their practice. The following are the major designations available to financial professionals, and some helpful information about each. Designations are listed in alphabetical order by acronym.

AAMS—ACCREDITED ASSET MANAGEMENT SPECIALIST

Awarded by the College for Financial Planning to investment professionals who complete a 12-module course, pass an exam, and agree to a code of ethics and to pursuing continuing education. AAMS is designed to enable the holder to identify opportunities not only in investments but also in the areas of insurance, tax, retirement, and estate planning, while making recommendations based on all aspects of a client's total financial picture. Contact:

College for Financial Planning
6161 South Syracuse Way
Greenwood Village, CO 80111
303-220-1200
<www.fp.edu>

AEP—ACCREDITED ESTATE PLANNER

Awarded by the National Association of Estate Planners & Councils to estate planners, attorneys, trust officers, and others who pass two graduate-level courses administered by The American College. Contact:

The American College
270 South Bryn Mawr Avenue
Bryn Mawr, PA 19010
610-526-1000
<www.amercoll.edu>

AFC—ACCREDITED FINANCIAL COUNSELOR

Granted by the Institute for Personal Finance, which is part of the Association for Financial Counseling and Education, the AFC designation requires completion of coursework and has ethics requirements. Contact:

Association for Financial Counseling and Education
2121 Arlington Avenue
Upper Arlington, OH 43221
614-485-9650

CDP—CERTIFIED DIVORCE PLANNER

A four-module correspondence course dealing with the financial aspects of divorce. After successful completion of tests at the end of each module, the financial professional receives a certificate and designation. Contact:

> Institute for Certified Divorce Planners
> 6395 Gunpark Drive
> Suite W
> Boulder, CO 80301
> 800-875-1760
> <www.institutecdp.com>

CFA—CHARTERED FINANCIAL ANALYST

These are investment advisors, securities analysts, and money managers who focus on securities analysis. They earn the CFA designation by completing a study course from the Association for Investment Management and Research (AIMR) and passing three annual examinations covering economics, financial accounting, portfolio management, securities analysis, and ethics. Contact:

> Association for Investment Management and Research
> P.O. Box 3668
> 560 Ray C. Hunt Drive
> Charlottesville, VA 22903-0668
> 800-247-8132
> <www.aimr.org>

CFP—CERTIFIED FINANCIAL PLANNER

Licensees of the Certified Financial Planner designation complete a college-level financial planning curriculum; take a ten-hour, two-day test; have at least three years of financial planning experience (if a college graduate); take 30 hours of continuing-education credits every two years; and adhere to the CFP Board's ethical standards. Contact:

Certified Financial Planner Board of Standards
1700 Broadway
Denver, CO 80290
303-830-7500
<www.cfp-board.org>

CFS—CERTIFIED FUND SPECIALIST

This designation, covering knowledge of mutual funds, requires taking a 60-hour course, passing an exam, adhering to a code of ethics, and completing 15 hours of continuing-education courses each year. Contact:

Institute of Business and Finance
7911 Herschel Avenue, Suite 201
La Jolla, CA 92037-4413
800-848-2029
<www.icfs.com>

CHFC—CHARTERED FINANCIAL CONSULTANT

After completing a ten-course financial planning curriculum from The American College and a two-hour exam, the candidate receives the ChFC designation. Contact:

The American College
270 South Bryn Mawr Avenue
Bryn Mawr, PA 19010
610-526-1000
<www.amercoll.edu>

CIMA—CERTIFIED INVESTMENT MANAGEMENT ANALYST

Awarded by the Investment Management Consultants Association, the CIMA designation requires passing a certifying exam, completing coursework at the Wharton School, having a minimum of three years of investment management consulting experience, and fulfilling continuing-education requirements. Contact:

Investment Management Consultants Association
9101 E. Kenyon Avenue, Suite 3000
Denver, CO 80237
303-770-3377
<www.imca.org>

CIMC—CERTIFIED INVESTMENT MANAGEMENT CONSULTANT

Awarded by the Institute for Certified Investment Management Consultants (ICIMC), the CIMC is held by consultants who work with clients and money managers, and who pass two levels of NASD-administered exams based on self-study courses, as well as meet ethical and experience requirements. Contact:

Institute for Certified Investment Management Consultants
1101 17th Street, N.W.
Washington, DC 20036

202-452-8670

<www.icimc.org>

CLU—CHARTERED LIFE UNDERWRITER

Certifying expertise in insurance, the CLU designation is awarded by The American College to financial services professionals who have met the three-year experience requirement, passed ten college-level education courses, and agreed to abide by a code of ethics. Contact:

The American College
270 South Bryn Mawr Avenue
Bryn Mawr, PA 19010
610-526-1000
<www.amercoll.edu>

CMFC—CHARTERED MUTUAL FUND COUNSELOR

The College for Financial Planning awards this designation to advisors who successfully complete a nine-module program sponsored by the College and the Investment Company Institute, agree to a code of ethics, and pursue continuing education. Contact:

College for Financial Planning
6161 South Syracuse Way
Greenwood Village, CO 80111
303-220-1200

CPA—CERTIFIED PUBLIC ACCOUNTANT

Awarded by the American Institute of Certified Public Accountants to those who pass the group's Uniform CPA Examination and satisfy state licensing requirements. Contact:

American Institute of Certified Public Accountants
1211 Avenue of the Americas
New York, NY 10036
212-596-6200
<www.aicpa.org>

CTFA—CERTIFIED TRUST AND FINANCIAL ADVISER

This designation is awarded by the Institute of Certified Bankers to those who meet personal trust experience and education requirements, pass an examination on tax law, investments, personal finance, fiduciary responsibilities, and trust activities, and agree to meet continuing-education requirements. Contact:

Institute of Certified Bankers
American Bankers Association
1120 Connecticut Avenue, N.W.
Washington, DC 20036
800-226-5377
<www.aba.com>

PFS—PERSONAL FINANCIAL SPECIALIST

The PFS designation is granted exclusively to CPAs with financial planning experience by the American Institute of Certified

Public Accountants. It requires passing a six-hour exam and pursuing continuing education. Contact:

> American Institute of Certified Public Accountants
> 1211 Avenue of the Americas
> New York, NY 10036
> 212-596-6200
> <www.aicpa.org>

RFC—REGISTERED FINANCIAL CONSULTANT

The International Association of Registered Financial Consultants awards the RFC designation to members who have met its education and experience requirements, and are licensed insurance or securities professionals. Contact:

> International Association of Registered Financial Consultants
> The Financial Planning Building
> 2507 North Verity Parkway
> Middletown, OH 45042
> 800-532-9060
> <www.iarfc.org>

Index